EXCELLER SELECT

TOP PICKS

PSYCHOSONIC

The Intersection of Music and Mental Health

PSYCHOSONIC

The Intersection of Music and Mental Health

OLANREWAJU O.H.

EXCELLER BOOKS®
A GLOBAL PRESS

PSYCHOSONIC
The Intersection of Music and Mental Health

Cover by Exceller Books using resources from Pixabay.com

ISBN: 978-93-48892-79-9

First published in India in 2024 by Exceller Books,
An imprint of GE Group

Address: G1, Dream Apartment, Degree College Road, Belgharia,
Kolkata, 700056, India
www.excellerbooks.com

EXCELLER BOOKS®
A GLOBAL PRESS

Dedication

To the Almighty God, the source of all wisdom, healing, and inspiration—this book is for Your glory.

To Celestial Church of Christ, El-Bethel Global Parish, Accra, Ghana—thank you for being my spiritual home and a place of divine encounter.

To my beloved Gracious Family on TikTok (I AM GRACIOUS)—your love, support, and connection have been a beacon of light on this journey. With gratitude and grace, —Olanrewaju.

Table of Contents

Introduction

Welcome to *Psychosonic: The Intersection of Music and Mental Health,* a profound exploration of the powerful connection between sound and the human psyche. In this book, we delve into the intricate ways music impacts our mental health, emotions, and overall well-being. Music, a universal language, transcends cultural and linguistic barriers, offering a unique window into the human experience. Through its rhythms, melodies, and harmonies, music has the profound ability to touch our souls, alter our moods, and heal our minds.

The Power of Sound

From the rhythmic beating of a drum to the soothing strains of a violin, sound has an inherent power to affect us on a deeply personal level. The ancients were aware of this; shamans, healers, and priests across various cultures utilised music and chants to heal the sick and communicate with the divine. Modern science is catching up, revealing how different frequencies and sound waves can stimulate brain activity, reduce stress, and even promote physical healing.

In the following chapters, we will explore:

- The science of sound: Understanding how sound waves interact with our brain and body.
- Therapeutic uses of music: From music therapy in clinical settings to self-administered musical interventions.
- Sound and emotion: How different types of music can evoke a wide range of emotional responses, from joy to sadness, excitement to calm.

The Universality of Music

Music is a global phenomenon. Every culture has its own unique musical traditions, yet the core elements of music—rhythm, melody, and harmony—are found everywhere. This universality suggests a deep-rooted connection between music and the human condition. Music speaks to something fundamental within us, bridging gaps between different cultures and creating shared experiences that foster empathy and understanding.

In this book, we will journey through:

- Global musical traditions: Examining the diverse ways different cultures use music in daily life, rituals, and celebrations.
- Cross-cultural studies: How music's universal aspects reveal commonalities in human emotion and cognition.
- Music and identity: The role of music in shaping personal and collective identities and how it can be used to express and process individual experiences.

The Intersection of Music and Mental Health

The central theme of this book is the intersection where music meets mental health. Music's capacity to influence our mental state is immense, offering a therapeutic avenue for managing mental health conditions like anxiety, depression, and PTSD. Through personal anecdotes, case studies, and scientific research, we will explore:

- Music as therapy: Success stories and methodologies from music therapy practitioners.
- Personal stories: Accounts from individuals who have used music to cope with mental health challenges.
- Scientific research: Insights from studies that highlight the effectiveness of music in mental health treatment.

Your Journey with Psychosonic

- *Psychosonic: The Intersection of Music and Mental Health* is not just a book to be read but an experience to be felt. As you turn the pages of this book, you will be invited to reflect on your own relationship with music and its impact on your mental and emotional well-being. We encourage you to engage with the music discussed, listen actively, and even create your own musical experiences as you explore the profound interplay between sound and the mind.

Join us on this enlightening journey into the heart of music's therapeutic power and its universal resonance. Discover how the sounds that surround us every day hold the potential to heal, inspire, and connect us all.

1 | Historical Perspectives on Music and Healing

Historical perspectives on music and healing take an intriguing turn when viewed through the lens of psychosonic theory, which explores the relationship between sound, consciousness, and healing. Throughout history, cultures worldwide have recognised the profound impact of sound on the human psyche, using music and sonic vibrations as tools for promoting physical, emotional, and spiritual well-being.

Ancient civilisations such as Egypt, Greece, and India understood the therapeutic potential of sound and music. In Egypt, hieroglyphs depict scenes of musicians playing instruments during healing rituals, while Greek philosophers, such as Pythagoras, explored the mathematical and harmonic principles underlying music's effects on the mind and body. In India, the practice of Nada Yoga involves using sound vibrations to achieve spiritual enlightenment and physical healing.

During the Middle Ages, the concept of psychosonic healing was evident in the use of Gregorian chants and sacred music in monastic settings. Monks believed that chanting specific melodies and hymns could invoke divine energies and bring about healing on a spiritual level.

The Renaissance period witnessed further exploration of psychosonic principles, with scholars such as Johannes Kepler and Robert Fludd delving into the connections between music, mathematics, and consciousness. Kepler, a renowned mathematician and astronomer, proposed that the harmony of the cosmos can be expressed through musical intervals, suggesting a deep interconnection between sound, geometry, and the human psyche.

In the 20th century, pioneers in the field of sound therapy, such as Alfred Tomatis and Hans Jenny, expanded upon psychosonic principles, exploring how specific frequencies and vibrations can affect mental and emotional states. Tomatis, for example, developed the concept of auditory integration training, using specially filtered music to stimulate the auditory system and improve various cognitive functions.

Today, psychosonic theory continues to inform practices in music therapy and holistic healing modalities. Therapists and practitioners harness the power of sound and music to induce states of relaxation, enhance self-awareness, and facilitate emotional release. From sound baths and vibrational healing sessions to personalised music therapy interventions, the ancient wisdom of psychosonic healing continues to resonate in modern approaches to health and well-being.

1.1. Defining Psychosonic: An Overview

Psychosonic is a term that merges the concepts of psychology and sonic (related to sound) to explore the intricate interplay between sound and the human mind. This interdisciplinary field encompasses elements from neuroscience, psychology, musicology, and acoustics to understand how sound affects mental states, emotions, cognition, and behaviour.

1.1.1. Historical Context

Interest in the relationship between sound and the human psyche is not a new phenomenon. Ancient civilisations utilised music and sound in rituals, healing practices, and communication. For instance, the Greeks believed in the ethos of music, where different modes could influence moral and emotional states. In the modern era, pioneers such as Alfred Tomatis and Oliver Sacks have made significant contributions to understanding how sound affects neurological and psychological functions.

1.1.2. Core Concepts

- Auditory Perception: This is the process by which the brain interprets and makes sense of the sounds we hear. It involves various brain regions and neural pathways that decode acoustic signals into meaningful information.
- Psychoacoustics: This branch of science examines the psychological responses evoked by sound. It explores how we perceive pitch, loudness, timbre, and spatial location of sounds and how these perceptions can evoke emotional and cognitive responses.
- Neurological Impact: Research in Psychosonic investigates how sound influences brain activity. Studies using EEG and fMRI have shown that different types of music and sounds can alter brain wave patterns, potentially affecting mood, concentration, and even physiological states such as heart rate and blood pressure.

1.1.3. Applications of Psychosonic Principles

- Music Therapy: By leveraging the therapeutic potential of music, music therapy utilises structured musical interventions to address the psychological, cognitive, and social needs of individuals. It has shown efficacy in treating conditions like depression, anxiety, and PTSD.
- Sound Design in Environments: The principles of psychosonic are applied in designing soundscapes for public spaces, workplaces, and healthcare settings to promote well-being, productivity, and comfort.
- Cognitive Enhancement: Certain frequencies and sound patterns, such as binaural beats, are used to enhance cognitive functions like focus, memory, and

creativity. These auditory stimuli can potentially entrain brain waves to desired states.

- Mindfulness and Relaxation: Sound is an integral part of practices like meditation and yoga. Specific sounds, such as gongs, singing bowls, and natural sounds, are used to facilitate relaxation and induce deep meditative states.

1.1.4. Scientific Research and Evidence

- Emotional Response to Music: Studies have shown that music can evoke strong emotional responses, which are measurable through physiological changes such as heart rate variability and galvanic skin response. Different genres and tempos can induce varying emotional states, from excitement to relaxation.
- Cognitive Function and Sound: Research indicates that background music can influence cognitive tasks. While some types of music can enhance concentration and task performance, others might be distracting. The 'Mozart Effect,' for example, suggests that listening to Mozart's music may temporarily enhance spatial-temporal reasoning abilities.
- Neuroplasticity: Ongoing research suggests that musical training and exposure can lead to neuroplastic changes in the brain, enhancing areas related to auditory processing, motor control, and even verbal memory.

1.1.5. Challenges and Future Directions

- Subjectivity of Sound Perception: One of the main challenges in psychosonic research is the subjective nature of sound perception. Individual differences in cultural background, personal preferences, and auditory health can significantly influence how sounds are perceived and their psychological impact.

- Interdisciplinary Integration: Psychosonic sits at the crossroads of multiple disciplines. Effective collaboration and integration of methodologies from neuroscience, psychology, and acoustics are crucial for advancing the field.
- Technological Advancements: Emerging technologies, such as virtual reality and advanced neuroimaging techniques, offer new avenues for exploring and applying psychosonic principles. These tools can provide more immersive and precise ways to study and utilise the effects of sound on the mind.

Psychosonic is an evolving field that underscores the profound connection between sound and the human mind. By bridging the gap between auditory experiences and psychological responses, it holds the potential to enhance mental health, cognitive function, and overall well-being. As research progresses and technological innovations continue, the applications of psychosonic principles are likely to expand, offering deeper insights and more effective interventions for harnessing the power of sound.

- Memory and Association: Music has a remarkable ability to evoke memories and mental imagery. This phenomenon, known as music-evoked autobiographical memory, involves the activation of brain regions associated with memory retrieval, such as the hippocampus and the medial prefrontal cortex. These regions link music to past experiences, imbuing it with personal significance.
- Reward System: Listening to music can be a pleasurable experience, thanks to the brain's reward system. When we hear music we enjoy, neurotransmitters like dopamine are released, triggering feelings of pleasure and reinforcing our connection to the music.
- Motor Regions: Beyond passive listening, actively engaging with music—whether through singing, playing instruments, or dancing—involves motor regions of the brain. These areas coordinate movement and rhythm, synchronising our body's actions with the music's tempo and beat.
- Attention and Executive Function: Music also captures our attention and engages executive functions of the brain, such as planning, problem-solving, and cognitive control. Musical training has been shown to enhance these cognitive abilities, promoting attentional focus and mental flexibility.
- Neuroplasticity: Finally, the brain's remarkable ability to adapt and reorganise in response to experience, known as neuroplasticity, plays a crucial role in how we process music. Musical training can reshape neural networks, strengthening connections between auditory, motor, and emotional regions of the brain.

The brain processes music through a complex interplay of auditory, emotional, memory, reward, motor, attentional, and neuroplasticity mechanisms. By unravelling these neural pathways, we gain insights into the profound impact that music has on our cognition, emotion, and behaviour.

2.2. Neurotransmitters and Mood Regulation

Neurotransmitters play a pivotal role in regulating mood and emotion, forming a critical link between psychosonic experiences—such as listening to music—and the brain's response. Understanding how neurotransmitters influence our emotional state sheds light on the profound effects of music on mood regulation.

- Dopamine: Often referred to as the feel-good neurotransmitter, dopamine is associated with pleasure, reward, and motivation. Listening to music that we enjoy can lead to the release of dopamine in the brain's reward pathways, eliciting feelings of pleasure and reinforcing our connection to the music. This dopamine release contributes to the uplifting and euphoric effects of music on mood.
- Serotonin is known as the neurotransmitter associated with happiness and plays a crucial role in regulating mood, sleep, and appetite. Music has been shown to increase serotonin levels in the brain, promoting feelings of relaxation, contentment, and overall well-being. This serotonin release contributes to the calming and stress-reducing effects of music, making it a valuable tool for managing anxiety and depression.
- Oxytocin: Often called the love hormone or bonding hormone, oxytocin is involved in social bonding, trust, and empathy. Music has the power to evoke strong emotional responses and foster a sense of connection with others, partly through the release of oxytocin. Shared musical experiences, such as singing in a choir or attending a concert, can promote feelings of closeness and belonging, enhancing social relationships and emotional resilience.

- Endorphins: Endorphins are natural painkillers produced by the brain in response to stress or discomfort. Music has been shown to stimulate the release of endorphins, leading to feelings of pleasure and relaxation. This endorphin release can reduce pain perception, alleviate stress, and promote a sense of well-being, making music an effective tool for managing pain and relieving stress.
- GABA (Gamma-Aminobutyric Acid): GABA is the brain's primary inhibitory neurotransmitter, involved in reducing neuronal excitability and promoting relaxation. Music has been found to increase GABA levels in the brain, leading to feelings of calmness and tranquillity. This GABAergic modulation contributes to the anxiolytic and stress-reducing effects of music, making it a valuable therapeutic tool for anxiety disorders and stress management.

Neurotransmitters play a crucial role in mediating the emotional effects of music on mood regulation. Through the release of dopamine, serotonin, oxytocin, endorphins, and GABA, music can evoke a wide range of emotional responses, from pleasure and relaxation to social bonding and pain relief. By understanding the neurochemical basis of music-induced mood modulation, we can harness the therapeutic potential of music to promote emotional well-being and enhance quality of life.

2.3. Case Studies: Music's Effect on the Brain

Music has long been recognised for its profound impact on human emotions and cognition—the emerging field of psychosonic delves deeper into understanding how music influences the brain and behaviour. Through case studies, we can examine the complex relationship between music and the psyche, illuminating its therapeutic, cognitive, and emotional effects.

2.3.1. Case Study 1: The Mozart Effect

In the early 1990s, psychologist Dr. Frances Rauscher conducted a study that suggested listening to Mozart's music could enhance spatial reasoning skills. The study sparked widespread interest in the Mozart effect, leading to further research on how specific musical elements stimulate neural pathways associated with cognitive functions. This case study highlights the potential of music to modulate brain activity and improve cognitive performance.

2.3.2. Case Study 2: Music Therapy in Alzheimer's Disease

Music therapy has emerged as a promising intervention for individuals with Alzheimer's disease and other forms of dementia. Case studies have documented remarkable outcomes, including enhanced mood, decreased agitation, and improved cognitive function among patients. By tapping into memory networks and emotional centres of the brain, music therapy demonstrates the power of music to transcend cognitive decline and connect individuals with their past experiences and identities.

2.3.3. Case Study 3: Rhythmic Entrainment in Parkinson's Disease

Parkinson's disease is characterised by motor symptoms such as tremors and rigidity, stemming from dopamine depletion in the brain. Research suggests that rhythmic auditory stimulation can enhance gait and movement coordination in individuals with Parkinson's disease. By synchronising movements with external rhythmic cues, such as music beats, individuals with Parkinson's can bypass dysfunctional neural circuits and facilitate smoother, more coordinated movements. This case study underscores the therapeutic potential of rhythmic entrainment in neurological disorders.

2.3.4. Case Study 4: Emotional Regulation through Music

Emotions are intricately linked to music, with certain melodies evoking specific emotional responses. Case studies have explored how music can serve as a powerful tool for emotional regulation, helping individuals manage stress, anxiety, and depression. By modulating activity in limbic regions of the brain, such as the amygdala and prefrontal cortex, music can induce relaxation, elevate mood, and promote emotional well-being. This case study highlights the role of music as a non-invasive and accessible intervention for emotional well-being.

Through case studies spanning diverse contexts, we gain deeper insights into the multifaceted effects of music on the brain and psyche. From enhancing cognitive function to alleviating symptoms of neurological disorders and promoting emotional well-being, music's influence extends far beyond mere auditory pleasure. As psychosonic continues to unravel the mysteries of music's impact, it holds promise for innovative interventions that harness the therapeutic potential of sound for human health and well-being.

3 | Psychological Responses to Music

Psychosonic is the study of psychological responses to music, encompassing the emotional, cognitive, and physiological effects music has on individuals. Here is some content exploring the fascinating relationship between music and the mind:

3.1. The Intricate Dance of Music and Psychology

Music holds the power to evoke a myriad of emotions, trigger memories, and even induce physical responses in listeners. This intricate dance between sound and psychology, known as psychosonic, sheds light on how music influences human behaviour, cognition, and emotions.

- Emotional Responses: One of the most evident effects of music on the mind is its ability to evoke emotions. Whether it is the euphoria of an upbeat melody or the melancholy of a soulful ballad, music has the uncanny ability to resonate with our innermost feelings. Psychosonic research delves into why certain musical elements, such as tempo, key, and harmonic structure, elicit specific emotional responses in listeners.
- Cognitive Impact: Beyond stirring emotions, music also affects cognitive processes, including attention, memory, and learning. For instance, background music has been shown to enhance concentration and productivity in some settings, while certain types of music can facilitate memory recall and learning in educational contexts. Psychosonic studies explore how music interacts with cognitive functions and its

potential applications in various domains, from education to therapy.

- Physiological Effects: The influence of music extends beyond the realm of thoughts and feelings to encompass physiological responses as well. Research has shown that listening to music can alter heart rate, blood pressure, and even respiratory patterns, indicating a direct link between auditory stimulation and bodily functions. Psychosonic investigates the mechanisms behind these physiological responses and their implications for health and well-being.
- Individual Differences: It is important to note that the psychological responses to music are highly individualised, shaped by factors such as personal experiences, cultural background, and musical preferences. What resonates deeply with one person may have little impact on another, highlighting the complexity of the psychosonic relationship. Understanding these individual differences is the key to harnessing the therapeutic potential of music in clinical settings.

Psychosonic offers a window into the intricate interplay between music and the human mind. By exploring the emotional, cognitive, and physiological responses to music, researchers gain valuable insights into how sound shapes our perceptions, behaviours, and overall well-being. Whether for therapeutic purposes, entertainment, or personal enrichment, the study of psychosonic continues to unravel the mysteries of our musical minds.

3.2. Emotional Resonance and Expression

Emotional resonance and expression are pivotal in the realm of psychosonic experiences, where the fusion of psychology and sound intertwines. Psychosonic exploration delves into how sound influences emotions and vice versa.

Emotional resonance occurs when certain sounds evoke deep feelings within us, stirring memories, triggering sensations, or eliciting profound emotional responses. These resonances can be highly individualised and influenced by personal experiences, cultural background, and psychological makeup. For example, a piece of music might evoke nostalgia for one person but sadness for another, depending on their unique associations with the melody or lyrics.

Expression within the psychosonic realm involves not only the creation of sound but also the interpretation and communication of emotions through it. Musicians, composers, and sound designers harness the power of tone, rhythm, and timbre to convey complex emotional landscapes. Similarly, listeners interpret and connect with music based on their own emotional experiences, forming a deeply personal relationship with the sonic artistry.

Through psychosonic exploration, individuals can gain insight into their emotions, uncover hidden feelings and gain a deeper understanding of themselves. This process of self-discovery can be therapeutic, offering a means of expression and catharsis. Moreover, the ability to recognise and articulate emotions through sound can enhance communication and empathy, fostering meaningful connections with others.

In essence, emotional resonance and expression within the realm of psychosonic offer a pathway to self-awareness, connection, and artistic innovation, bridging the gap between the auditory and emotional realms of human experience.

3.3. Music Therapy: Techniques and Practices in Relation to Psychosonic Therapy

Music therapy is the clinical and evidence-based use of music interventions to accomplish individualised goals within a therapeutic relationship. This approach leverages the psychological and emotional power of music to address physical, emotional, cognitive, and social needs. When integrated with psychosonic therapy, music therapy becomes an even more potent tool, utilising sound frequencies and music to impact the mind and body holistically.

3.3.1. Techniques in Music Therapy

3.3.1.1. Receptive Music Therapy

- Listening Sessions: Patients listen to music selected by the therapist to elicit emotional responses or to facilitate relaxation and stress reduction.
- Music-Assisted Relaxation: Combining music with relaxation techniques like progressive muscle relaxation, guided imagery, or deep breathing.

3.3.1.2. Active Music Therapy

- Improvisation: Encouraging patients to create spontaneous music using instruments or their voices can help them express emotions and enhance their creativity.
- Songwriting: Collaboratively writing songs with the therapist to express feelings, tell personal stories, or develop coping strategies.
- Instrument Playing: Using instruments to explore and express emotions, improve motor skills, and increase social interaction.

3.3.1.3. Clinical Techniques

- Lyric Analysis: Discussing the lyrics of songs to help patients explore their thoughts and feelings and to facilitate dialogue about personal issues.
- Rhythmic Auditory Stimulation (RAS): Using rhythmic cues to improve motor control and coordination, especially in patients with neurological conditions like Parkinson's disease or stroke.

3.3.2. Psychosonic Practices

Psychosonic therapy combines elements of psychology and acoustics to use sound for therapeutic purposes. This practice emphasises the influence of sound frequencies and music on mental states, emotions, and physical well-being.

3.3.2.1. Sound Frequency Healing

- Binaural Beats: Utilising slightly different frequencies played in each ear to alter brain wave patterns, promoting relaxation, focus, or sleep.
- Solfeggio Frequencies: Using specific frequencies believed to have healing properties, such as 528 Hz for DNA repair and 432 Hz for emotional grounding.

3.3.2.2. Vibroacoustic Therapy

- Sound and Vibration: Patients lie on a special bed or chair that emits sound vibrations, which can help reduce pain, improve circulation, and promote relaxation.

3.3.2.3. Tuning Fork Therapy

- Frequency Application: Applying specific frequencies via tuning forks to the body's energy points to promote healing and balance.

3.3.4. Integration of Music Therapy and Psychosonic Techniques

3.3.4.1. Holistic Soundscapes

- Customised Music Programs: Creating personalised music and sound programs that integrate specific frequencies known to support mental health and physical healing.
- Therapeutic Sound Journeys: Guiding patients through immersive sound experiences that combine

music, nature sounds, and therapeutic frequencies to promote deep relaxation and emotional release.

3.3.4.2. Mindfulness and sound meditation

- Mindful Listening: Combining mindfulness practices with attentive listening to therapeutic music or soundscapes to enhance emotional regulation and mental clarity.
- Gong Baths and Singing Bowls: Using these instruments in meditation sessions to create a deep, resonant sound that promotes relaxation and spiritual connection.

3.3.4.3. Biofeedback and Music

- Real-Time Feedback: Using biofeedback devices to monitor physiological responses and adjust the music in real-time to optimise therapeutic outcomes.
- Interactive Sessions: Patients interact with music and sound based on their biofeedback data, which can help them understand and regulate their emotional and physiological states.

Music therapy and psychosonic practices, when combined, offer a comprehensive approach to healing that addresses the mind, body, and spirit. By employing a variety of techniques and practices, therapists can create personalised and effective interventions that leverage the profound impact of music and sound on human health and well-being. These therapies not only provide relief from various conditions but also empower individuals to connect with their emotions and improve their quality of life through the universal language of music.

3.4. Psychological Theories and Models in Relation to Psychosonic Therapy

Psychosonic therapy is an interdisciplinary approach that blends principles from psychology and acoustics to leverage sound for therapeutic purposes. The integration of psychological theories and models into psychosonic therapy enhances its efficacy by grounding sound interventions in well-established psychological frameworks. Here is a detailed exploration of how various psychological theories and models relate to and inform psychosonic therapy.

3.4.1. Cognitive-Behavioural Theory (CBT)

Application in Psychosonic Therapy:

Cognitive Restructuring with Music: Music can be used to facilitate cognitive restructuring by helping clients reframe negative thoughts and emotions. Listening to uplifting or calming music can change mood states and promote positive thinking patterns.

Behavioural Activation: Incorporating music into daily routines to increase engagement in enjoyable activities, thereby reducing symptoms of depression and anxiety.

Example: Using music with positive lyrical content during therapy sessions to challenge and change maladaptive thoughts and behaviours.

3.4.2. Psychodynamic Theory

Application in Psychosonic Therapy:

- Unconscious Exploration: Soundscapes and music can evoke unconscious memories and emotions, facilitating the exploration and processing of repressed material.
- Transference and Countertransference: Music can serve as a medium through which transference and countertransference dynamics are explored, thereby deepening the therapeutic relationship.

Example: Using improvised music sessions allows clients to express unconscious feelings and conflicts.

3.4.3. Humanistic Theory

Application in Psychosonic Therapy:

- Self-Actualisation: Music and sound can be tools for self-discovery and personal growth, helping individuals achieve self-actualisation.
- Empathy and Unconditional Positive Regard: Creating a non-judgmental space with supportive and empathic music selections that resonate with clients' emotional states.

Example: Employing client-preferred music to build rapport and facilitate self-exploration and authenticity in therapy.

3.4.4. Neuroplasticity and Neuroscience Models

Application in Psychosonic Therapy:

- Brainwave Entrainment: Using binaural beats and other sound frequencies to entrain brainwaves, promoting relaxation, focus, and cognitive flexibility.
- Neuroplastic Changes: Engaging clients in music-based activities stimulates brain regions associated with memory, emotion, and motor control, thereby fostering neuroplasticity.

Example: Utilising rhythmic auditory stimulation (RAS) to improve motor functions in patients with neurological impairments.

3.4.5. Biopsychosocial Model

Application in Psychosonic Therapy:

- Holistic Approach: Addressing biological, psychological, and social factors by incorporating sound and music interventions that impact emotional and physical health.

- Stress Reduction: Utilising music and sound to manage stress, which in turn positively impacts physical health and social functioning.

Example: Creating personalised soundscapes for stress management that consider the individual's biological responses, psychological needs, and social context.

3.4.6. Attachment Theory

Application in Psychosonic Therapy:

- Secure Attachment through Music: Using music to create a sense of safety and security fosters secure attachment relationships in therapeutic settings.
- Emotional Bonding: Facilitating emotional bonding between therapist and client through shared musical experiences.

Example: Using lullabies and soothing music to help individuals with attachment issues develop a sense of security and trust.

3.4.7. Existential Theory

Application in Psychosonic Therapy:

- Exploration of Meaning: Engaging clients in music that prompts reflection on existential themes such as meaning, death, freedom, and isolation.
- Authenticity and Presence: Encouraging clients to use music as a means to explore and express their authentic selves and to be fully present in the moment.

Example: Using existentially themed music to facilitate discussions about life purpose and personal values.

Integrating psychological theories and models into psychosonic therapy provides a robust framework for understanding and leveraging the therapeutic potential of sound. By aligning sound-based interventions with established psychological principles, therapists can create more effective and holistic treatment plans. This interdisciplinary approach not only enhances the therapeutic process but also offers clients a richer, more nuanced pathway to healing and personal growth.

4 | Music and Cognitive Function

Music has long been recognised for its profound impact on human emotions and physical well-being. Recent research has expanded this understanding to encompass its significant influence on cognitive functions. From enhancing memory and attention to improving executive function and language skills, music offers a powerful tool for cognitive development and rehabilitation. Here, we explore how music interacts with various aspects of cognitive function.

4.1. Memory Enhancement

- Mechanisms:
    - ✓ Encoding and Retrieval: Music aids in encoding and retrieval processes. Melodic and rhythmic structures of music create strong mnemonic devices, making information more accessible.
    - ✓ Association: Associative learning through music links information with familiar tunes or lyrics, facilitating easier recall.
- Applications:
    - ✓ Educational Settings: Using songs and musical mnemonics to help students memorise information like the alphabet, historical facts, or mathematical formulas.
    - ✓ Therapeutic Interventions: Using music therapy for patients with Alzheimer's or other forms of dementia to trigger memories and improve cognitive function.

Example: Patients with Alzheimer's disease often recall personal memories when they hear music from their past, demonstrating music's powerful effect on memory retrieval.

4.2. Attention and concentration

- Mechanisms
  - ✓ Arousal and Regulation: Music regulates arousal levels, helping individuals maintain optimal alertness and focus.
  - ✓ Cognitive Load Management: Background music can mask environmental distractions, allowing for better concentration on tasks.
- Applications
  - ✓ Work and Study Environments: Playing background music to enhance productivity.
  - ✓ ADHD Management: Using rhythmic and structured music to improve attention spans in individuals with ADHD.

Example: Students studying with classical or instrumental music often report higher levels of concentration and productivity compared to studying in silence or with lyrics-heavy music.

4.3. Executive Function

- Mechanisms
  - ✓ Improved Cognitive Flexibility: Music training enhances cognitive flexibility, allowing individuals to switch between tasks more efficiently.
  - ✓ Inhibitory Control: Learning to play an instrument requires practice and discipline, which strengthens inhibitory control and self-regulation.
- Applications
  - ✓ Cognitive Rehabilitation: Incorporating music training into programs designed to improve

executive function in individuals recovering from brain injuries.
  - ✓ Developmental Benefits: Music education for children supports the development of executive functions, aiding in school readiness and academic performance.

Example: Children who participate in music lessons tend to exhibit better performance in tasks that require executive function, such as problem-solving and planning.

4.4. Language and Verbal Skills

- Mechanisms
  - ✓ Prosody and Rhythm: Music enhances the understanding of prosody and rhythm in speech, aiding in language acquisition and fluency.
  - ✓ Auditory Discrimination: Musical training improves auditory discrimination, which is crucial for language development and phonological awareness.
- Applications
  - ✓ Language Learning: Using songs and rhythmic activities to teach new languages and improve pronunciation and fluency.
  - ✓ Speech Therapy: Incorporating musical elements into speech therapy for individuals with language impairments.

Example: Children learning a second language through songs and musical games often show accelerated improvement in vocabulary and pronunciation.

4.5. Emotional and Social Cognition

- Mechanisms
  - ✓ Emotional Recognition: Music helps in recognising and interpreting emotions, both in oneself and others, enhancing emotional intelligence.

- ✓ Social Bonding: Group musical activities foster social interaction and cooperation, strengthening social cognition and empathy.
- Applications
  - ✓ Group Therapy: Using group music-making activities to improve social skills and emotional understanding in individuals with autism or social anxiety.
  - ✓ Emotional Regulation: Employing music to help individuals manage and regulate their emotions effectively.

Example: Individuals participating in choir singing report increased feelings of social connectedness and improved emotional regulation.

The influence of music on cognitive function is multifaceted and profound. From enhancing memory and attention to supporting executive function and language skills, music serves as a versatile tool in both educational and therapeutic contexts. By leveraging the cognitive benefits of music, educators, therapists, and individuals can foster cognitive development and improve overall mental functioning, making music not just an art form but a powerful ally in cognitive enhancement and rehabilitation.

4.6. Enhancing Memory and Learning in Relation to Music and Cognitive Function

Music has a profound impact on cognitive functions, including memory and learning. Numerous studies have demonstrated that music can enhance memory retention, facilitate learning processes, and improve overall cognitive performance. This relationship between music and cognitive function can be harnessed in educational and therapeutic contexts to maximise benefits.

4.7. Mechanisms of Music in Enhancing Memory and Learning

4.7.1. Encoding and Retrieval

- Mnemonic Devices: Music can act as a powerful mnemonic tool. The rhythmic and melodic patterns in music make information more memorable. For example, songs or rhymes can help encode and recall complex information.
- Contextual Cues: Music provides contextual cues that aid in memory retrieval. Associating a particular piece of music with certain information can trigger recall when the same music is played later.

4.7.2. Emotional Engagement

- Mood Regulation: Music can help regulate mood, reducing anxiety and stress that can otherwise hinder learning and memory processes. A positive emotional state is conducive to better learning and retention.
- Motivation: Music increases motivation and engagement, making learning activities more enjoyable and thus more effective.

4.7.3. Neuroplasticity

- Brain Activation: Music stimulates multiple brain regions involved in memory, attention, and executive function. This activation promotes neuroplasticity, enhancing cognitive abilities and learning capacity.
- Synaptic Strengthening: Repeated exposure to music strengthens synaptic connections, facilitating the consolidation of memory and enhancing recall.

4.8 Applications in Educational Settings

4.8.1. Classroom Strategies

- Musical Mnemonics: Teachers can utilise songs or rhythmic patterns to aid students in remembering information. For example, the "ABC" song helps children learn the alphabet.

- Background Music: Playing instrumental music during study sessions can enhance focus and reduce distractions, thereby facilitating better information absorption.

4.8.2. Language Learning

- Phonetic Awareness: Music enhances phonetic awareness, a crucial component for language acquisition. Singing in a new language helps with pronunciation, vocabulary, and fluency.
- Cultural Context: Incorporating culturally relevant music into language learning offers contextual insights and enhances the learning experience.

4.8.3. Memory Retention Techniques

- Repetition and Variation: Repeating information through different musical formats (songs, raps, and rhymes) reinforces learning and memory retention.
- Association: Linking new information to familiar melodies or rhythms creates strong memory associations, making recall easier.

4.9. Applications in Therapeutic Settings

4.9.1. Dementia and Alzheimer's Disease

- Music Therapy: Music therapy can stimulate cognitive function and evoke memories in patients with dementia. Familiar songs can trigger autobiographical memories and improve cognitive engagement.
- Daily Routines: Incorporating music into daily routines helps maintain cognitive functions and enhances the quality of life for individuals with dementia.

4.9.2. Stroke Rehabilitation

- Neurologic Music Therapy (NMT): Using rhythm and melody to improve cognitive and motor functions in stroke patients. Techniques like Rhythmic Auditory Stimulation (RAS) help in regaining motor control and cognitive processing.
- Memory Exercises: Structured musical activities designed to enhance memory recall and cognitive function are part of rehabilitation programs.

4.9.3. Learning Disabilities

- Adaptive Music Programs: Customised music programs for individuals with learning disabilities can improve memory, attention, and learning outcomes. Music therapy provides alternative pathways for learning and memory retention.
- Multi-Sensory Learning: Combining visual, auditory, and kinesthetic learning styles with music caters to different learning needs and enhances overall cognitive development.

4.9.3.1. Case Studies and Examples

- Educational Success: A study showed that elementary students who learned multiplication tables through songs outperformed those who used traditional memorisation techniques.
- Therapeutic Outcomes: Music therapy sessions with Alzheimer's patients led to improved mood, increased social interaction, and enhanced memory recall of personal events when specific songs from their youth were played.
- Language Acquisition: Research indicates that adult language learners who incorporated singing into their study routine had better pronunciation and

vocabulary recall compared to those who used standard study methods.

The impact of music on memory and learning is significant and multifaceted. By engaging various cognitive processes, music not only makes learning more enjoyable but also more effective. In both educational and therapeutic contexts, the strategic use of music can enhance memory retention, learning efficiency, and overall cognitive function. Leveraging the power of music provides a holistic approach to cognitive development and rehabilitation, benefiting educators, therapists, and learners alike.

4.10. Music's Role in Cognitive Rehabilitation

Cognitive rehabilitation is a therapeutic approach designed to help individuals regain cognitive functioning lost due to neurological conditions, brain injuries, or mental health disorders. One increasingly recognised tool in cognitive rehabilitation is music. Music therapy and related interventions harness the power of music to stimulate brain function, enhance memory, and improve emotional well-being. Here is an overview of how music plays a pivotal role in cognitive rehabilitation:

4.10.1. Stimulating Brain Function

Music activates multiple areas of the brain, including those involved in emotion, memory, and motor control. Listening to or playing music can stimulate neural pathways and promote neuroplasticity, the brain's ability to reorganise itself by forming new neural connections. This is crucial for individuals recovering from brain injuries, strokes, or neurodegenerative diseases.

4.10.2. Enhancing Memory and Learning

Music can aid in memory recall and improve learning abilities. Familiar melodies and rhythms can evoke memories and emotions, making it easier for patients to access and retrieve information. In cognitive rehabilitation, music is often used to create mnemonic devices or to structure repetitive learning tasks, aiding in the retention of new information.

4.10.3. Improving Attention and Focus

Engaging with music requires sustained attention and focus. Music therapy exercises often involve tasks that require attention to rhythm, melody, and harmony, thereby enhancing cognitive control and concentration. This can be particularly beneficial for individuals with attention deficits or cognitive impairments resulting from brain injuries.

4.10.4. Reducing Anxiety and Depression

Music has a profound impact on emotional well-being. It can reduce stress, alleviate anxiety, and lift mood. These emotional benefits are crucial in cognitive rehabilitation, as they can enhance a patient's motivation and engagement in other therapeutic activities. A positive emotional state is conducive to learning and cognitive recovery.

4.10.5. Facilitating Speech and Language Recovery

For individuals with aphasia or other language impairments, music can be a powerful tool. Melodic intonation therapy (MIT), which utilises the musical elements of speech, such as melody and rhythm, aids patients in improving their speech production. Singing and rhythmic speech patterns can bypass damaged areas of the brain and engage alternative neural pathways for communication.

4.10.6. Enhancing Motor Skills and Coordination

Music therapy can also address motor deficits. Rhythmic auditory stimulation (RAS) uses the rhythm in music to improve gait and coordination in individuals with motor impairments. For example, stroke patients or individuals with Parkinson's disease often show improvements in walking speed, stride length, and overall coordination when engaging in music-based exercises.

4.10.7. Promoting Social Interaction

Music often involves collaborative activities, such as group singing, playing in a band, or music-based games. These activities can enhance social skills, reduce feelings of isolation, and provide a sense of community and support. Social interaction is a crucial aspect of cognitive rehabilitation, significantly contributing to overall mental health and quality of life.

Music's multifaceted impact on the brain makes it a valuable component of cognitive rehabilitation. Its ability to stimulate neural activity, enhance memory, improve attention, reduce anxiety, aid in language recovery, and promote motor skills and social interaction highlights its versatility as a therapeutic tool. As research continues to uncover the mechanisms behind music's effects on the brain, its application in cognitive rehabilitation is likely to expand, offering hope and improved outcomes for many individuals facing cognitive challenges.

4.11. Case Studies: Cognitive Improvements through Music

Music has long been a subject of interest in the study of cognitive improvement and brain function. Numerous case studies have shown that music can significantly enhance cognitive abilities, including memory, attention, problem-solving, and even emotional intelligence. This document explores several case studies that highlight the impact of music on cognitive development and functioning.

4.11.1. Case Study 1: Music and Memory Enhancement

- Participants and Methods: A study conducted by the University of California involved 60 participants aged 65–80, divided into two groups. One group participated in music lessons (learning to play the piano) for six months, while the control group did not engage in any musical activity.

- Findings: The results demonstrated that the group involved in music lessons showed a significant improvement in memory retention and recall abilities. Neuroimaging revealed increased activity in the hippocampus, a region of the brain associated with memory. These findings suggest that engaging in musical activities can help mitigate age-related cognitive decline.

4.11.2. Case Study 2: Music and Language Development in Children

- Participants and Methods: Researchers at the University of Toronto conducted a study involving 50 children aged 4 to 6 years. The children were divided into two groups; one group received music training (choir and instrumental lessons), while the other group received visual arts training for one year.
- Findings: The children in the music training group showed enhanced linguistic abilities, including improved vocabulary and grammar skills. Brain scans revealed increased activity in the left temporal lobe, a region associated with language processing. This study highlights the potential of music education in early childhood to foster language development.

4.11.3. Case Study 3: Music Therapy for Cognitive Rehabilitation

- Participants and Methods: A study at the Beth Israel Deaconess Medical Centre involved 30 stroke patients undergoing cognitive rehabilitation. Half of the patients received standard rehabilitation, while the other half received music therapy, which included listening to and playing music.

- Findings: Patients in the music therapy group showed greater improvements in cognitive functions such as attention, problem-solving, and executive functioning compared to those receiving standard rehabilitation. The study concluded that music therapy can be a valuable adjunct to traditional cognitive rehabilitation methods for stroke patients.

4.11.4. Case Study 4: The Mozart Effect

- Participants and Methods: A landmark study conducted by researchers at the University of California, Irvine, explored the short-term cognitive effects of listening to Mozart's music. College students were divided into three groups: one listened to Mozart's sonata, another to relaxation instructions, and the third to silence.
- Findings: The group that listened to Mozart's music scored higher on spatial-temporal reasoning tasks immediately after the listening session compared to the other two groups. This phenomenon, known as the Mozart Effect, suggests that listening to certain types of music can temporarily enhance cognitive abilities.

4.11.5. Case Study 5: Music and Emotional Intelligence

- Participants and Methods: A study by Goldsmiths, University of London, involved 100 adults who were assessed for emotional intelligence (EI) levels. The participants were then divided into two groups: one received music training, and the other received no intervention over a period of six months.
- Findings: The group that underwent music training showed a marked increase in emotional intelligence scores, particularly in areas of empathy and emotional

regulation. This suggests that music training can contribute to the development of emotional intelligence, a crucial aspect for social interactions and personal well-being.

The case studies presented demonstrate the diverse and profound impact of music on cognitive functions. From memory enhancement and language development to rehabilitation and emotional intelligence, music proves to be a powerful tool in improving various aspects of cognition. These findings underscore the importance of integrating music education and therapy into educational and healthcare settings to leverage their cognitive benefits.

5 | Clinical Applications of Music Therapy

Music therapy is a clinical and evidence-based practice that utilises music interventions to achieve individualised goals within a therapeutic relationship. It has been shown to address a wide range of physical, emotional, cognitive, and social needs. This document examines the diverse clinical applications of music therapy, highlighting its effectiveness in various healthcare settings.

5.1. Music Therapy in Mental Health Treatment

Music therapy has demonstrated significant benefits in treating mental health conditions such as depression, anxiety, and PTSD.

- Depression and Anxiety: Music therapy can help reduce symptoms of depression and anxiety by promoting relaxation, improving mood, and providing an outlet for emotional expression. Studies have shown that patients participating in music therapy sessions exhibit reduced levels of cortisol (a stress hormone) and increased production of serotonin and dopamine, neurotransmitters associated with well-being and happiness.
- Post-Traumatic Stress Disorder (PTSD): For individuals with PTSD, music therapy can offer a safe space to process traumatic memories and emotions. Techniques such as songwriting, improvisation, and listening to calming music can help patients manage symptoms and improve their quality of life.

5.2. Music Therapy in Neurological Rehabilitation

Music therapy is widely used in the rehabilitation of patients with neurological disorders, including stroke, traumatic brain injury (TBI), and Parkinson's disease.

- Stroke Rehabilitation: Music therapy can aid in the recovery of motor and cognitive functions following a stroke. Techniques such as rhythmic auditory stimulation (RAS) are used to enhance gait and motor coordination, while melodic intonation therapy (MIT) helps individuals regain their speech and language abilities.
- Traumatic Brain Injury (TBI): For TBI patients, music therapy can enhance cognitive functions, including attention, memory, and executive functioning. It can also support emotional regulation and social interaction, contributing to overall recovery.
- Parkinson's Disease: Patients with Parkinson's disease often benefit from music therapy through improved motor function, reduced bradykinesia (slowness of movement), and enhanced emotional well-being. Rhythmic auditory cues can help patients improve their walking speed and balance.

5.3. Music Therapy in Pain Management

Music therapy is an effective non-pharmacological intervention for pain management in various clinical settings, including chronic pain conditions and postoperative care.

- Chronic Pain: Patients with chronic pain conditions such as fibromyalgia and arthritis can benefit from music therapy through distraction, relaxation, and emotional support. Listening to and creating music can reduce the perception of pain and improve coping mechanisms.
- Postoperative Pain: In postoperative care, music therapy can reduce pain and anxiety, leading to a

decreased need for analgesics. Patients who listen to music before, during, and after surgery often report lower pain levels and higher overall satisfaction with their surgical experience.

5.4. Music Therapy in Paediatric Care

Music therapy is particularly effective in paediatric settings, addressing both the physical and psychological needs of children.

- Hospitalised Children: For children in hospitals, music therapy can reduce anxiety, alleviate pain, and provide a sense of normalcy. Interactive music activities, such as playing instruments or singing, can distract children from medical procedures and create a more positive hospital experience.
- Developmental Disorders: Children with developmental disorders, such as autism spectrum disorder (ASD) and attention-deficit/hyperactivity disorder (ADHD), can benefit from music therapy through improved communication, social skills, and emotional regulation. Structured music activities can help these children develop essential life skills in an engaging and motivating way.

5.5. Music Therapy in Palliative and Hospice Care

In palliative and hospice care, music therapy provides emotional support, pain relief, and enhanced quality of life for patients and their families.

- Emotional and Spiritual Support: Music therapy can help patients and their families cope with the emotional and spiritual challenges of end-of-life care. Music can provide comfort, evoke meaningful memories, and facilitate emotional expression.
- Symptom Management: Music therapy can also aid in managing symptoms such as pain, anxiety, and

shortness of breath. By creating a calming environment, music can help patients achieve a sense of peace and relaxation.

Music therapy is a versatile and effective clinical intervention that addresses a wide range of health issues across various populations. Its applications in mental health, neurological rehabilitation, pain management, paediatric care, and palliative care highlight its potential to improve patients' physical, emotional, and cognitive well-being. As research continues to support its benefits, music therapy is becoming an increasingly integral part of holistic healthcare practices.

5.6. Music Therapy in Mental Health Settings

Music therapy is a well-established clinical practice that utilises the therapeutic potential of music to address mental health issues. By integrating musical elements and techniques within a therapeutic framework, music therapy facilitates emotional expression, psychological processing, and overall mental well-being. This document explores the applications, techniques, and benefits of music therapy in mental health settings.

5.6.1. Applications of Music Therapy in Mental Health

Music therapy is used to treat a variety of mental health conditions, including depression, anxiety, post-traumatic stress disorder (PTSD), schizophrenia, and bipolar disorder. It serves both as a primary intervention and as an adjunct to other forms of therapy.

- Depression: Music therapy can help alleviate symptoms of depression by fostering emotional expression and enhancing mood. Participating in musical activities, such as songwriting or playing instruments, allows patients to process and express their feelings. Listening to uplifting or soothing music can also promote a sense of well-being and reduce depressive symptoms.

- Anxiety: For individuals with anxiety disorders, music therapy offers a non-verbal outlet for stress and anxiety reduction. Techniques such as guided imagery with music (GIM) and relaxation exercises set to calming music can help lower physiological arousal, leading to reduced anxiety levels. Active participation in music-making can also distract from anxious thoughts and promote mindfulness.
- PTSD: Music therapy provides a safe space for individuals with PTSD to process traumatic experiences. Techniques such as improvisation, drumming, and songwriting help patients externalise and make sense of their trauma. Music can also help regulate emotions and foster a sense of safety and grounding.
- Schizophrenia: Patients with schizophrenia can benefit from music therapy through improved social interaction, emotional expression, and cognitive functioning. Group music therapy sessions encourage social engagement and communication, while structured musical activities can enhance concentration and reduce psychotic symptoms.
- Bipolar Disorder: Music therapy helps individuals with bipolar disorder manage mood swings and stabilise emotions. Creating and listening to music can serve as a coping mechanism during manic or depressive episodes. Music therapy also aids in developing routine and structure, which is beneficial for mood regulation.

5.7. Techniques in Music Therapy

Music therapists employ a variety of techniques tailored to the needs and preferences of their clients. These techniques include both active and receptive methods.

5.7.1. Active Techniques

- Improvisation: Clients create spontaneous music using instruments or their voices, facilitating self-expression and emotional release.
- Songwriting: Clients compose lyrics and melodies, which can help articulate thoughts and feelings that are difficult to express verbally.
- Instrument Play: Playing instruments offers a tactile and auditory means of expression, enhancing motor skills and coordination.
- Singing: Singing familiar songs can evoke positive memories and emotions, while vocal exercises can improve breathing and relaxation.

5.7.2. Receptive Techniques

- Listening: Clients listen to pre-recorded or live music selected by the therapist to evoke specific emotional or cognitive responses.
- Guided Imagery with Music (GIM): Clients listen to music while being guided through imagery exercises, promoting relaxation and insight.
- Music-Assisted Relaxation: Combining music with progressive muscle relaxation or deep breathing exercises to reduce stress and induce calm.

5.8. Benefits of Music Therapy for Mental Health

Music therapy offers numerous benefits that contribute to mental health and well-being.

5.8.1. Emotional Expression and Regulation

Music therapy provides a non-verbal medium for expressing complex emotions, enabling clients to process and manage their feelings effectively. This can be particularly beneficial for those who struggle to express their emotions solely through words.

5.8.2. Stress Reduction

Engaging with music has been shown to lower cortisol levels, the hormone associated with stress. Techniques such as music-assisted relaxation and guided imagery promote a state of calm and relaxation, reducing overall stress levels.

5.8.3. Enhanced Mood

Listening to or creating music can trigger the release of endorphins and dopamine, neurotransmitters linked to pleasure and happiness. This can lead to improved mood and a reduction in symptoms of depression and anxiety.

5.8.4. Improved Social Interaction

Group music therapy sessions foster social connection and communication skills. Shared musical experiences can create a sense of community and belonging, which is particularly valuable for individuals who experience social isolation.

5.8.5. Cognitive Benefits

Music therapy can enhance cognitive functions, including attention, memory, and executive functioning. Structured musical activities stimulate brain regions involved in these cognitive processes, contributing to overall mental acuity.

Music therapy is a versatile and effective intervention in mental health settings, offering a range of benefits for individuals with various mental health conditions. Through tailored musical activities and therapeutic techniques, music therapy fosters emotional expression, reduces stress, enhances mood, and improves cognitive and social functioning. As an integral part of holistic mental health care, music therapy continues to demonstrate its profound impact on mental wellness and quality of life.

5.9. Techniques for Anxiety and Depression: Clinical Applications of Music Therapy

Music therapy is an evidence-based clinical practice that utilises musical interventions to enhance mental health and well-being. It has been shown to be particularly effective in treating anxiety and depression, offering a unique way to address emotional, cognitive, and social needs. Here are several techniques and their clinical applications in managing anxiety and depression:

5.9.1. Active Music Making

- Instrumental Improvisation
  - ✓ Overview: It involves playing instruments spontaneously to express emotions and thoughts.
  - ✓ Clinical Application: It helps individuals explore and process feelings, reduce stress, and enhance emotional expression. For example, drumming can serve as an outlet for releasing tension and frustration.
- Singing
  - ✓ Overview: Engaging in vocal activities, either solo or in groups.
  - ✓ Clinical Application: Singing can improve mood and increase feelings of social connectedness. It promotes deep breathing, which can reduce anxiety, and the act of vocalising can release endorphins and oxytocin, enhancing mood and social bonding.

5.9.2. Receptive music listening

- Guided Imagery and Music (GIM)
  - ✓ Overview: A therapeutic technique that uses music to evoke imagery, facilitating deeper emotional exploration and insight.
  - ✓ Clinical Application: It helps individuals access and process subconscious emotions, reduce anxiety, and promote relaxation. It can be particularly useful for exploring and addressing the underlying causes of depression.

- Music-Assisted Relaxation
  - ✓ Overview: Listening to pre-recorded or live music selected to promote relaxation and reduce stress.
  - ✓ Clinical Application: It helps lower physiological arousal, reduce muscle tension, and promote a sense of calm. Soft, slow-tempo music is often used to facilitate relaxation and improve sleep quality, which is crucial for individuals with anxiety and depression.

5.9.3. Songwriting and Lyric Analysis

- Songwriting
  - ✓ Overview: Creating original songs or altering existing ones to express personal experiences and emotions.
  - ✓ Clinical Application: It provides a creative outlet for expressing feelings and thoughts, facilitating emotional processing and catharsis. It can help individuals articulate complex emotions related to anxiety and depression in a structured and meaningful way.
- Lyric Analysis

- ✓ Overview: Discussing and interpreting the lyrics of songs that resonate with the individual's experiences.
- ✓ Clinical Application: It helps individuals connect with and articulate their emotions, gain insights into their experiences, and foster a sense of validation and understanding. It can also be used to challenge negative thought patterns and reinforce positive messages.

5.9.4. Rhythmic Entrainment

- Drumming Circles
  - ✓ Overview: Group drumming sessions that involve synchronised rhythms.
  - ✓ Clinical Application: It promotes social interaction, reduces feelings of isolation, and enhances mood through collective rhythmic activities. The repetitive and rhythmic nature of drumming can also induce a meditative state, helping to reduce anxiety.
- Heartbeat Rhythm Exercises
  - ✓ Overview: Using rhythms that mimic the natural heartbeat to promote a sense of security and calm.
  - ✓ Clinical Application: It helps regulate emotions and reduce anxiety by creating a steady, comforting rhythm that individuals can attune to, thereby stabilising their internal states.

5.9.5. Music and Movement

- Dance/Movement Therapy
  - ✓ Overview: Combining music with movement to promote emotional, social, cognitive, and physical integration.

  - ✓ Clinical Application: It helps individuals express emotions non-verbally, release tension, and improve body awareness. Movement to music can also enhance mood and energy levels, counteracting the lethargy often associated with depression.
- Tai Chi with Music
  - ✓ Overview: Integrating Tai Chi exercises with calming music to enhance relaxation and mindfulness.
  - ✓ Clinical Application: It improves physical and mental well-being, reduces stress, and promotes relaxation through slow, deliberate movements coordinated with soothing music. This combination can be particularly effective in reducing symptoms of anxiety.

Music therapy offers a versatile and holistic approach to managing anxiety and depression. Through active music making, receptive listening, songwriting, rhythmic entertainment, and music and movement, individuals can discover new ways to express their emotions, reduce stress, and enhance their overall mental well-being. Clinical applications of music therapy not only address the symptoms of anxiety and depression but also promote emotional expression, social connection, and personal insight, making it a valuable tool in the therapeutic arsenal.

5.10. Music and PTSD: Healing Trauma

Post-Traumatic Stress Disorder (PTSD) affects millions worldwide, resulting from experiencing or witnessing traumatic events. Symptoms include flashbacks, severe anxiety, and uncontrollable thoughts about the event. While traditional treatments like therapy and medication are commonly used, music has emerged as a powerful tool for healing trauma.

5.10.1. The Healing Power of Music

Music therapy has gained recognition for its therapeutic benefits in treating PTSD. It leverages music's ability to evoke emotions, alter moods, and provide a non-verbal outlet for expression. Here are some ways music aids in healing trauma:

- Emotional Expression: Music allows individuals to express feelings that are difficult to verbalise. For PTSD sufferers, who often struggle with talking about their experiences, music can provide a safe medium for emotional release.
- Stress Reduction: Listening to calming music can lower cortisol levels, reducing stress and anxiety. Music with a slow tempo, in particular, helps slow down the heart rate and promote relaxation.
- Memory and Processing: Music can trigger memories and emotions, enabling individuals to process their trauma in a controlled and therapeutic environment. This can be especially useful in therapeutic settings where guided music sessions are used to address specific traumatic memories.
- Improved Mood and Motivation: Engaging with music, whether through listening, singing, or playing an instrument, can elevate mood and provide a sense of achievement. This can be particularly beneficial for those with PTSD, who may often feel hopeless or detached.
- Social Connection: Group music therapy sessions foster a sense of community and support among participants. Shared musical experiences can help build connections and reduce the feelings of isolation common in PTSD.

5.11. Applications of Music Therapy for PTSD

- Guided Imagery and Music (GIM): This technique involves listening to music while guided imagery helps individuals explore and process their traumatic experiences. GIM sessions are typically led by trained therapists who use specific music to evoke emotional responses and facilitate healing.

- Songwriting: Creating music allows individuals to tell their stories and regain a sense of control. Songwriting can be a cathartic experience, helping to externalise trauma and foster resilience.
- Instrumental Play: Playing instruments can be a powerful way to release pent-up emotions. The physical act of creating music can also enhance motor skills and serve as a constructive outlet for stress and anxiety.
- Music Listening: Personalised playlists can be used to manage symptoms. For instance, calming music can help reduce anxiety, while upbeat tracks can combat depression and lethargy.

5.12. Scientific Evidence

Research supports the efficacy of music therapy in treating PTSD. Studies have shown that music can activate areas of the brain associated with emotion and memory, aiding in the processing of traumatic experiences. Furthermore, music therapy has been linked to reductions in PTSD symptoms, such as anxiety and depression, and improvements in overall quality of life.

Although music therapy is not a standalone cure for PTSD, it is a valuable complement to traditional treatments. Its ability to provide emotional relief, reduce stress, and foster social connections makes it a powerful tool in the healing process. For individuals suffering from PTSD, music can be a beacon of hope, offering a path to recovery through creativity and expression.

6 | Personalized Music Therapy

6.1. Tailoring Sound for Healing

Music therapy has long been recognised for its therapeutic benefits, offering a unique approach to healing and emotional expression. Personalised music therapy takes this a step further by customising the musical experience to fit an individual's specific needs, preferences, and therapeutic goals. This tailored approach maximises the effectiveness of music therapy, ensuring that each session resonates deeply with the participant.

6.2. What Is Personalized Music Therapy?

Personalised music therapy involves designing music interventions that cater to the unique characteristics of an individual. This includes considering their musical tastes, cultural background, emotional state, and specific health conditions. By aligning the therapy with personal preferences and needs, therapists can create a more impactful and meaningful healing experience.

6.3. Benefits of Personalized Music Therapy

- Enhanced Engagement: When music therapy is personalised, individuals are more likely to engage with the process. Familiar and preferred music can capture attention and evoke strong emotional responses, making the therapy sessions more effective.
- Emotional Resonance: Music that resonates with a person's life experiences and emotional state can evoke deeper emotional responses. This facilitates the

expression and processing of emotions, which is crucial for healing.

- Cultural Relevance: Incorporating music that reflects an individual's cultural background can make therapy more relatable and effective. This cultural sensitivity can help build trust and comfort between the therapist and the participant.
- Targeted Therapeutic Goals: Personalised music therapy can be tailored to address specific therapeutic goals, such as reducing anxiety, improving mood, enhancing cognitive function, or aiding in physical rehabilitation. This focused approach ensures that the therapy is aligned with the individual's health objectives.
- Improved Outcomes: Studies have shown that personalised music therapy can lead to better therapeutic outcomes compared to generic music interventions. This includes improvements in emotional well-being, cognitive function, and physical health.

6.4. How Personalized Music Therapy Works

- Assessment: The process begins with a thorough assessment of the individual's needs, preferences, and health conditions. This may involve interviews, questionnaires, and discussions with healthcare providers.
- Selection of Music: Based on the assessment, therapists select music that aligns with the individual's tastes and therapeutic goals. This can include specific genres, artists, or songs that hold personal significance to the individual.
- Customised Interventions: Therapists design music interventions tailored to the individual. This can include listening sessions, guided imagery,

songwriting, instrumental play, or movement to music.

- Ongoing Evaluation: The effectiveness of the therapy is continually evaluated, with adjustments made as needed to ensure optimal outcomes. Feedback from the individual is crucial in refining the therapy.

6.5. Applications of Personalized Music Therapy

- Mental Health: Personalised music therapy can be particularly effective for individuals with mental health conditions such as depression, anxiety, PTSD, and bipolar disorder. Tailored music can help regulate emotions, reduce stress, and improve mood.
- Neurological Disorders: For conditions like Alzheimer's, Parkinson's, and stroke, personalised music therapy can enhance cognitive function, improve motor skills, and boost overall quality of life. Familiar music can stimulate memory and encourage movement.
- Pain Management: Customised music therapy can help manage chronic pain by providing a distraction, reducing stress, and promoting relaxation. Music can alter pain perception and enhance the effectiveness of pain relief strategies.
- Rehabilitation: In physical rehabilitation, personalised music therapy can motivate individuals to engage in exercises and improve their physical abilities. Rhythmic music, in particular, can enhance coordination and motor function.

Personalised music therapy represents a powerful and flexible approach to healing, offering a deeply resonant and effective form of therapy. By aligning with individual preferences and therapeutic goals, it maximises the potential benefits of music as a therapeutic tool. Whether addressing mental health issues, neurological disorders, pain management, or physical rehabilitation, music therapy provides a unique pathway to wellness and recovery.

6.6. Assessing Individual Needs and Preferences in Personalized Music Therapy

Personalised music therapy tailors interventions to fit an individual's unique characteristics, maximising therapeutic outcomes. A critical component of this approach is a thorough assessment of individual needs and preferences. This process ensures that the selected music and therapeutic activities are most effective and meaningful to the participant.

6.6.1. Importance of Assessment

The assessment phase is crucial in personalised music therapy as it:

- Identifies Specific Needs: Understanding the individual's health conditions, emotional state, and therapeutic goals allows for targeted interventions.
- Ensures Relevance: Selecting music that resonates with the individual's personal and cultural background enhances engagement and therapeutic impact.
- Maximises Effectiveness: Customising therapy based on detailed assessments can lead to more significant and quicker improvements in health and well-being.

6.6.2. Components of a Comprehensive Assessment

- Medical and Psychological History: Reviewing the individual's medical and psychological background helps identify areas where music therapy can be beneficial. This includes understanding any diagnoses, treatments, and existing symptoms.
- Therapeutic Goals: Discussing with the individual (and caregivers, if applicable) to set clear, achievable goals. Goals may include reducing anxiety, managing

pain, improving mood, enhancing cognitive function, or aiding physical rehabilitation.

- Musical Preferences: Gathering detailed information about the individual's musical tastes, including favourite genres, artists, songs, and any specific memories or emotions associated with certain music.
- Cultural and Social Background: Understanding the individual's cultural, religious, and social background ensures the music selected is respectful and relevant. This can include traditional music, hymns, or culturally significant songs.
- Current Emotional and Mental State: Assessing the individual's current emotional and mental state helps tailor the music to support their immediate needs, such as calming music for anxiety or uplifting tunes for depression.
- Physical Abilities and Limitations: Evaluating the individual's physical condition is essential for designing appropriate musical activities. For instance, rhythm-based exercises that develop motor skills or gentle movement to music can be beneficial for individuals with physical limitations.

6.6.3. Methods of Assessment

- Interviews: Conducting interviews with the individual and, if applicable, their family members or caregivers, helps gather qualitative information about their history, preferences, and goals.
- Questionnaires and Surveys: Utilising standardised tools to collect information on musical preferences, emotional responses to music, and perceived benefits of music therapy.
- Observations: Observing the individual's reactions to different types of music and activities during initial

sessions helps refine the therapeutic approach based on real-time feedback.

- Collaboration with Healthcare Providers: Working with doctors, psychologists, and other healthcare professionals helps understand the individual's medical and psychological needs and integrate music therapy into their overall treatment plan.

6.6.4. Implementing Findings into Therapy

- Customised Music Selection: Using the assessment data to create personalised playlists and select music for therapeutic sessions that resonate with the individual's tastes and therapeutic needs.
- Designing Tailored Interventions: Developing specific music therapy activities, such as guided imagery with music, songwriting, instrumental play, or movement to music, that align with the individual's goals and capabilities.
- Continuous Monitoring and Adaptation: Regularly evaluating the individual's progress and adjusting the therapy as needed. This includes seeking feedback and making necessary changes to the music or activities to ensure ongoing effectiveness.

Assessing individual needs and preferences is a foundational step in personalised music therapy. By thoroughly understanding the individual's medical background, therapeutic goals, musical tastes, cultural context, and current emotional and physical state, therapists can design highly effective and meaningful interventions. This tailored approach not only enhances engagement and relevance but also maximises the therapeutic benefits of music, providing a unique and powerful pathway to healing and well-being.

6.7. Creating Personalized Treatment Plans in Personalized Music Therapy

Personalised music therapy involves crafting treatment plans that are tailored to the unique needs, preferences, and therapeutic goals of each individual. These customised plans ensure that music interventions are not only effective but also meaningful and engaging for the participant. Here is a detailed look at how personalised treatment plans are created in the context of music therapy:

6.7.1. Importance of Personalized Treatment Plans

- Targeted Therapy: By addressing specific needs and goals identified during assessment, personalised treatment plans focus on achieving measurable outcomes. This can include reducing symptoms of anxiety or depression, improving cognitive function, enhancing emotional expression, or facilitating physical rehabilitation.
- Individualised Approach: Recognising that each person responds differently to music, personalised treatment plans adapt music interventions to suit the individual's musical preferences, cultural background, emotional state, and cognitive abilities.
- Engagement and Motivation: When therapy aligns with personal interests and preferences, individuals are more likely to actively participate and remain engaged throughout the treatment process. This enhances motivation and supports consistent progress.
- Holistic Integration: Personalised treatment plans integrate music therapy seamlessly into the individual's overall care regimen, collaborating with other healthcare providers and aligning with existing treatments or therapies.

6.7.2. Components of a Personalized Treatment Plan

- Goals and Objectives: Clearly defining therapeutic goals based on the individual's assessment. Goals should be specific, measurable, achievable, relevant, and time-bound (SMART), such as reducing symptoms of PTSD, improving mood stability, or enhancing social interaction skills.
- Music Selection: Choosing music that resonates with the individual's preferences and therapeutic goals. This may include favourite songs, genres, or styles that evoke positive emotions or memories, promote relaxation, or stimulate cognitive functions.
- Therapeutic Activities: Designing activities that utilise music to achieve therapeutic outcomes. Examples include:
  - ✓ Listening Sessions: Creating personalised playlists for relaxation, mood regulation, or reminiscence.
  - ✓ Songwriting: Encouraging the individual to express emotions and experiences through lyrics and melody.
  - ✓ Instrumental Play: Using instruments to improve fine motor skills, coordination, and sensory integration.
  - ✓ Movement to Music: Engaging in rhythmic exercises or dance movements to enhance physical coordination and emotional expression.
- Progress Monitoring: Establishing methods to assess and track progress towards treatment goals. This may involve regular evaluations, feedback sessions, and adjustments to the treatment plan based on observed outcomes and the individual's responses.
- Collaboration and Communication: Maintaining open communication with the individual, their caregivers, and other healthcare providers involved in their care.

This ensures that the music therapy plan complements other treatments and addresses holistic well-being.

6.7.3. Implementation and Adjustment

- Initial Sessions: Introducing the personalised treatment plan during initial therapy sessions, explaining the rationale behind selected activities and music choices. This sets expectations and fosters a collaborative approach between the therapist and the participant.
- Adaptation and Flexibility: Remaining flexible to adjust the treatment plan based on the individual's progress, changing needs, and feedback. Modifications may include altering music selections, refining therapeutic techniques, or exploring new activities to better meet therapeutic goals.
- Long-term Planning: Developing a long-term roadmap for therapy, with milestones and checkpoints to review progress and adjust treatment objectives as the individual achieves goals or faces new challenges.

Creating personalised treatment plans in personalised music therapy is essential for optimising therapeutic outcomes. By customising goals, music selections, and therapeutic activities to align with individual preferences and needs, therapists can enhance engagement, motivation, and the overall effectiveness of music as a therapeutic tool. This holistic approach not only supports emotional, cognitive, and physical well-being but also empowers individuals to actively participate in their healing journey through the transformative power of music.

6.8. Measuring Outcomes and Effectiveness in Personalised Music Therapy

Measuring outcomes and effectiveness in personalised music therapy involves assessing how well the therapy achieves its intended goals and impacts the individuals receiving it. Here are key aspects to consider when evaluating personalised music therapy:

- Goal Setting and Measurement: Effective personalised music therapy begins with clearly defined goals tailored to the individual's needs. These goals can range from improving mood and reducing anxiety to enhancing cognitive function or social interaction. Each goal should be measurable and specific, allowing therapists to track progress over time.
- Quantitative Assessments: Objective measures such as standardised scales for anxiety, depression, cognitive function, or quality of life are commonly used to quantify changes before, during, and after therapy sessions. These assessments provide numerical data that can indicate the effectiveness of personalised music interventions.
- Qualitative Feedback: Qualitative feedback from participants, caregivers, and therapists is essential in understanding the subjective experiences and perceived benefits of personalised music therapy. Interviews, surveys, and structured feedback sessions can reveal insights into emotional responses, improvements in communication, or changes in behaviour.
- Neuroscientific Measures: Advances in neuroimaging techniques, such as functional MRI (fMRI) or EEG, can provide objective insights into how personalised music therapy affects brain activity and neural pathways. These measures help elucidate mechanisms of action and validate therapeutic approaches.
- Longitudinal Studies: Long-term studies tracking participants over extended periods can assess the sustainability of benefits gained from personalised music therapy. Longitudinal data can also highlight

any long-lasting effects on mood, cognition, or quality of life.

- Comparative Studies: Comparing personalised music therapy with other therapeutic approaches or control groups can elucidate its unique contributions and effectiveness relative to alternative interventions. Randomised controlled trials (RCTs) are particularly valuable for establishing causality and confirming therapeutic efficacy.
- Cost-Benefit Analysis: Evaluating the economic impact of personalised music therapy involves assessing healthcare costs, hospitalisation rates, medication use, and overall healthcare utilisation before and after therapy. Cost-benefit analyses can demonstrate potential savings associated with improved health outcomes.
- Ethical Considerations: Ensuring ethical practices in research and therapy involves respecting participant autonomy, ensuring informed consent, maintaining confidentiality, and addressing any potential conflicts of interest. Ethical guidelines uphold the integrity and credibility of personalised music therapy research.

By integrating these approaches, researchers and clinicians can comprehensively evaluate the outcomes and effectiveness of personalised music therapy. This holistic assessment not only validates its therapeutic benefits but also informs future advancements and applications in healthcare settings.

7 | Innovative Practices in Music Therapy

Music therapy, the clinical and evidence-based use of music interventions to accomplish individualised goals within a therapeutic relationship, has seen numerous innovative practices in recent years. These innovations enhance its effectiveness and accessibility, expanding the boundaries of how music can be used to heal and improve the quality of life. Here are some of the most notable innovations in the field:

7.1. Technological Integration

The incorporation of technology into music therapy has opened up new possibilities. From virtual reality (VR) experiences to specialised music therapy apps, technology is making therapy more engaging and accessible.

- Virtual Reality (VR): VR creates immersive environments that can be tailored to the needs of the client, providing new avenues for emotional expression and sensory engagement. VR music therapy is being used for patients with anxiety, PTSD, and chronic pain.
- Music Therapy Apps: There are numerous apps designed for music therapy that allow for interactive and personalised music creation. These apps can be used in and out of therapy sessions, providing continuous support.

7.2. Telehealth and Online Music Therapy

The rise of telehealth has revolutionised access to music therapy. Online sessions make it possible for clients who live in remote areas or have mobility issues to receive therapy.

- Remote Sessions: Using video conferencing tools, therapists can conduct sessions that include live music, songwriting, and musical improvisation.
- Online Resources: There is a growing library of online resources, including instructional videos and digital instruments, making music therapy more accessible than ever.

7.3. Neurologic Music Therapy (NMT)

NMT is an evidence-based approach that uses music to achieve non-musical goals, specifically those related to neurological functions. It is used for patients with conditions such as stroke, traumatic brain injury, and Parkinson's disease.

- Rhythmic Auditory Stimulation (RAS): RAS utilises the rhythm in music to enhance motor control, particularly in gait and movement.
- Melodic Intonation Therapy (MIT): This therapy utilises the musical elements of speech to enhance language skills in patients with aphasia.

7.4. Community Music Therapy

Community Music Therapy (CoMT) moves beyond traditional therapy settings to engage with communities, promoting social change and community well-being through collective music-making.

- Group Sessions: Group drumming circles, choirs, and band formations help build social connections and a sense of community.

- Public Performances: Clients often participate in public performances, which can help enhance their self-esteem and promote community integration.

7.5. Cultural Sensitivity and Inclusivity

Music therapists are increasingly recognising the importance of cultural sensitivity in their practice. This includes incorporating culturally relevant music and understanding the cultural contexts of their clients.

- Culturally Relevant Repertoire: Using music that is meaningful and familiar to clients from diverse cultural backgrounds.
- Cultural Competence Training: Therapists undergo training to better understand and respect the cultural backgrounds and preferences of their clients.

7.6. Personalized Music Therapy

With advancements in data collection and analysis, therapists can now create highly personalised music therapy programs.

- Biometric Feedback: By utilising biometric data (such as heart rate and brain waves), therapists can tailor music interventions to the physiological and emotional needs of clients in real-time.
- AI and Machine Learning: These technologies are being explored to develop personalised playlists and interventions based on individual preferences and therapeutic goals.

7.7. Interdisciplinary Approaches

Music therapy is increasingly integrated with other therapeutic modalities, providing a holistic approach to treatment.

- Music and Mindfulness: Combining music therapy with mindfulness practices to enhance relaxation and stress reduction.

- Music and Cognitive Behavioural Therapy (CBT): Using music to complement CBT techniques, making therapy more engaging and effective.

Innovative practices in music therapy are continuously evolving, driven by technological advancements, increased accessibility, and a deeper understanding of the human brain and behaviour. These innovations are not only enhancing the effectiveness of music therapy but also making it more inclusive and personalised, offering new hope and healing to individuals across various populations.

7.8. Technological Advancements in Innovative Music Therapy Practices

Music therapy, a field dedicated to the therapeutic use of music, has undergone significant evolution with the advent of new technologies. These advancements have expanded the scope, accessibility, and efficacy of music therapy, enabling therapists to offer more personalised and effective treatments. Here are some key technological innovations shaping modern music therapy practices:

7.8.1. Digital Music Platforms and Apps

The proliferation of digital music platforms and therapeutic apps has revolutionised the accessibility of music therapy. Apps like SingFit, Meludia, and Insight Timer provide therapeutic exercises and guided music therapy sessions that patients can access remotely. These platforms use algorithms to tailor music selections and activities to the individual needs of the users, making therapy more personalised and effective.

7.8.2. Virtual Reality (VR) and Augmented Reality (AR)

VR and AR technologies are being used to create immersive therapeutic environments. VR can transport patients to calming, virtual spaces where they can interact with music in a controlled, multi-sensory environment. This is particularly beneficial for patients with anxiety, PTSD, and other mental health conditions. For instance, VR therapy can simulate a concert or a nature walk with accompanying therapeutic music, providing a powerful tool for relaxation and emotional processing.

7.8.3. Biofeedback and Neurofeedback

Biofeedback and neurofeedback technologies measure physiological and neural responses to music in real-time. Devices such as heart rate monitors, EEGs, and skin conductance sensors provide data on how a patient's body and brain respond to music therapy. This data can help therapists adjust sessions in real-time to optimise therapeutic outcomes. For example, if a patient's heart rate decreases while listening to a particular type of music, that music can be used more frequently in therapy.

7.8.4. AI and Machine Learning

Artificial intelligence and machine learning are being employed to create adaptive music therapy programs. These technologies can analyse large datasets of patient responses to various musical elements and predict the most effective therapeutic strategies for new patients. AI can also generate personalised music compositions that cater to the specific emotional and psychological needs of individuals, enhancing the therapeutic process.

7.8.5. Telehealth and Online Sessions

The rise of telehealth has made music therapy more accessible to people in remote or underserved areas. Online video conferencing tools allow therapists to conduct sessions remotely, breaking geographical barriers. This has proven particularly valuable during times when in-person sessions are not possible, such as during the COVID-19 pandemic.

7.8.6. Interactive Music Technology

Innovative instruments and devices, such as MIDI controllers and digital interfaces, enable patients to create and interact with music in new and engaging ways. These tools can be particularly empowering for individuals with physical disabilities, as they often require minimal physical effort to produce music. Interactive music technology can also be used in group settings, fostering social interaction and collaboration among patients.

7.8.7. Sound and Music Analysis Software

Advanced software for sound and music analysis enables therapists to understand the intricate details of music that can significantly influence therapeutic outcomes. Programs like Sonic Visualiser and Audacity allow therapists to analyse the frequency, tempo, and structure of music to select the most effective pieces for therapy. This analytical approach ensures that the therapeutic use of music is both scientifically grounded and highly targeted.

7.8.8. Wearable Technology

Wearable devices such as smartwatches and fitness trackers can monitor patients' physiological responses during music therapy sessions. This device-driven approach enables continuous monitoring and tracks key metrics, including heart rate variability, stress levels, and sleep patterns, providing valuable insights into the therapeutic impact of music. This data, combined with adjustments to therapy, helps meet the evolving needs of patients.

The integration of technology into music therapy is transforming the field, making it more personalised, accessible, and effective. From digital platforms and VR to AI and wearable technology, these innovations are enhancing the way music therapy is delivered and experienced. As technology continues to advance, the potential for new and innovative therapeutic practices in music therapy will only continue to expand, offering new hope and possibilities for patients worldwide.

7.9. Integrating Music with Other Therapies

Music therapy has long been recognised for its therapeutic benefits, harnessing the power of music to enhance physical, emotional, cognitive, and social well-being. The integration of music therapy with other therapeutic modalities represents a dynamic and innovative approach that can amplify the benefits of both music and the accompanying therapies. Here, we explore some of the cutting-edge practices and their applications.

7.9.1. Music Therapy and Cognitive Behavioral Therapy (CBT)

Combining music therapy with CBT can be particularly effective in treating anxiety, depression, and PTSD. Music can serve as a medium to express emotions and thoughts that are difficult to articulate verbally. Techniques such as songwriting, guided imagery with music, and lyric analysis can complement CBT's focus on changing negative thought patterns, making the therapeutic process more engaging and accessible.

- Innovative Practice Example: A music therapist collaborates with a CBT therapist to create personalised playlists that align with the client's cognitive restructuring goals. During sessions, clients may listen to these playlists while engaging in CBT exercises, which helps reinforce positive thinking and relaxation.

7.9.2. Music Therapy and Physical Therapy

Music's rhythm and tempo can significantly enhance physical therapy outcomes. Rhythmic auditory stimulation (RAS) is a technique where rhythmic cues are used to improve gait and movement in patients with Parkinson's disease, stroke, or traumatic brain injury. The synchronisation of movement to music can enhance motor skills, coordination, and endurance.

- Innovative Practice Example: Incorporating interactive music technology, such as motion-capture systems, that respond to patients' movements to create real-time music feedback. This can motivate patients to engage more fully in physical therapy exercises, improving their rehabilitation outcomes.

7.9.3. Music Therapy and Occupational Therapy

Music can be a powerful tool in occupational therapy to improve fine motor skills, cognitive functions, and sensory processing. Music activities, such as playing instruments, singing, and dancing to music, can enhance hand-eye coordination, attention span, and sensory integration.

- Innovative Practice Example: Using adaptive musical instruments and digital music apps that allow patients with limited mobility or cognitive impairments to participate actively in music-making, thereby improving their engagement and outcomes in occupational therapy sessions.

7.9.4. Music Therapy and Speech-Language Therapy

Music and speech are closely related in the brain, making music therapy an effective adjunct to speech-language therapy. Techniques such as melodic intonation therapy (MIT) utilise the musical elements of speech to enhance language production in patients with aphasia or other speech disorders.

- Innovative Practice Example: Developing software applications that combine speech exercises with musical elements, such as pitch and rhythm, to create a fun and motivating platform for patients to practise their speech and language skills.

7.9.5. Music Therapy and Psychotherapy

Music therapy can deepen the psychotherapeutic process by accessing emotions and memories that may not be easily reached through traditional talk therapy. Music improvisation, songwriting, and music-assisted relaxation can facilitate emotional expression, processing of traumatic experiences, and overall emotional regulation.

- Innovative Practice Example: Implementing virtual reality (VR) environments where clients can engage in music therapy sessions that provide immersive experiences tailored to their therapeutic needs. This can create a safe space for exploring difficult emotions and experiences.

7.9.6. Music Therapy and Alternative Therapies

Integrating music therapy with complementary therapies, such as mindfulness, yoga, and acupuncture, can create a holistic approach to health and wellness. Music can enhance the effects of these therapies by promoting relaxation, reducing stress, and improving mood.

- Innovative Practice Example: Designing multi-sensory environments where music, aromatherapy, and visual stimuli are combined to create a comprehensive therapeutic experience. These environments can be used for relaxation, stress reduction, and pain management.

The integration of music therapy with other therapeutic modalities represents a promising frontier in holistic health care. These innovative practices not only enhance the effectiveness of traditional therapies but also create more engaging and personalised treatment experiences. As research in this field continues to grow, we can expect to see even more creative and effective ways to incorporate music into diverse therapeutic practices.

7.10. Future Directions in Music Therapy

As the field of music therapy continues to evolve, several exciting future directions are emerging. These trends promise to expand the scope and effectiveness of music therapy, integrating new technologies, research methodologies, and interdisciplinary approaches to enhance therapeutic outcomes. Here are some key areas where music therapy is poised to grow and innovate.

7.10.1. Technological Integration

- Virtual Reality (VR) and Augmented Reality (AR): The integration of VR and AR technologies into music therapy can create immersive therapeutic environments. These technologies can simulate calming landscapes or interactive musical experiences, providing a safe and engaging space for clients to explore emotions, reduce anxiety, and practise new skills.
- Wearable Technology: Wearable devices that monitor physiological responses such as heart rate, stress levels, and movement can provide real-time data to tailor music therapy interventions. For instance, biofeedback devices can help therapists adjust music to synchronise with the client's physiological state, enhancing the therapeutic effect.
- Artificial Intelligence (AI): AI can be used to create personalised music therapy sessions. Algorithms can analyse a client's preferences, emotional responses, and progress to suggest specific musical pieces or therapeutic activities. AI-driven applications can also facilitate remote music therapy sessions, making therapy more accessible.

7.10.2. Neuroscientific Research

Advancements in neuroscience are providing deeper insights into how music affects the brain. Future research will likely focus on mapping out the neural mechanisms underlying music therapy, and identifying how different elements of music (rhythm, melody, harmony) impact various brain regions and cognitive functions. This knowledge can lead to more precise and effective music therapy techniques.

7.10.3. Personalized Music Therapy

Personalised medicine is a growing trend in healthcare, and music therapy is no exception. Future music therapy practices will likely be highly individualised, taking into account a client's genetic makeup, personality, cultural background, and specific health conditions. Tailoring music therapy to these factors can enhance its efficacy and relevance

7.10.4. Interdisciplinary Approaches

Collaboration between music therapists and professionals from other fields, such as psychology, neurology, physical therapy, and education, is expected to grow. Interdisciplinary teams can develop comprehensive treatment plans that address the multifaceted needs of clients. For example, music therapists working with neurorehabilitation teams can create integrated interventions that combine motor, cognitive, and emotional therapies.

7.10.5. Community and Social Impact

Music therapy can play a significant role in community health and social change. Future directions may include more community-based programs that use music to address public health issues, promote social cohesion, and support marginalised populations. For instance, music therapy programs in schools, prisons, and refugee camps can provide emotional support and foster a sense of belonging.

7.10.6. Expanded Applications

As research continues to validate the benefits of music therapy, its applications are likely to expand into new areas. Emerging fields include:

- Chronic Pain Management: Music therapy is increasingly recognised for its ability to reduce chronic pain and improve quality of life for individuals with conditions like fibromyalgia and arthritis.
- Neurodevelopmental Disorders: Innovative music therapy techniques are being developed to support individuals with autism spectrum disorders, ADHD, and other neurodevelopmental conditions, focusing on improving communication, social skills, and executive functioning.
- Ageing and Dementia Care: With an ageing population, there is growing interest in using music therapy to support cognitive function, reduce agitation, and improve the well-being of individuals with dementia and other age-related conditions.

7.10.7. Advocacy and Policy Development

The future of music therapy will also involve greater advocacy for the profession and the development of policies that support its integration into mainstream healthcare. Efforts to secure insurance coverage, standardise certification processes, and promote public awareness will be crucial in expanding access to music therapy services.

The future of music therapy is bright, with numerous opportunities for growth and innovation. By embracing new technologies, advancing neuroscientific research, personalising interventions, fostering interdisciplinary collaboration, expanding applications, and advocating for the profession, music therapy can continue to enhance the health and well-being of individuals and communities worldwide.

8 | Cultural Perspective on Music and Healing

Music has been intertwined with healing practices across diverse cultures for millennia. Various societies have recognised and harnessed the therapeutic potential of music to promote physical, emotional, and spiritual well-being. Here is a detailed exploration of how different cultures perceive and utilise music for healing:

- *Indigenous Cultures:* Indigenous communities worldwide have long incorporated music into their healing rituals and ceremonies. For example:
  - ✓ Native American Traditions: In Native American culture, music plays a central role in healing ceremonies. Drumming, singing, and chanting are used to connect with the spiritual realm, seeking guidance and intervention from ancestors and nature spirits. These practices aim to restore harmony and balance within individuals and the community.
  - ✓ Aboriginal Australian Healing: The Didgeridoo, an ancient wind instrument, is traditionally used in Aboriginal Australian healing ceremonies. Its deep, resonant sounds are believed to align the energies of the body, promoting physical and spiritual healing.
- Asian Traditions: Asian cultures have developed sophisticated systems in which music plays a vital role in promoting health and well-being.
  - ✓ Chinese Medicine: In Traditional Chinese Medicine (TCM), the concept of "healing

sounds" is pivotal. Each organ is associated with specific sounds that can help balance the body's Qi (vital energy). For example, the sound "shhh" is believed to aid the liver, promoting calm and reducing anger.

- ✓ Indian Ayurveda: In Ayurveda, the ancient Indian system of medicine, music therapy, known as "Nada Yoga," uses specific ragas (melodic frameworks) to influence the chakras (energy centres) and doshas (body constitutions). Different ragas are played at various times of the day to harmonise the body and mind.

- African Traditions: In many African cultures, music and dance are inseparable from healing practices.
  - ✓ West African Drumming: In West African traditions, drumming circles are used for healing. The rhythms and beats of the drums are believed to communicate with the spiritual world, invoking protective and healing spirits. This communal activity promotes emotional release and social cohesion, both of which are essential for overall well-being.
  - ✓ Sangoma Healers: In Southern Africa, Sangoma healers use music, dance, and chanting in their healing rituals. These practices are designed to connect with ancestors and facilitate the flow of healing energies, addressing both physical ailments and psychological distress.
- Middle Eastern Traditions: The Middle East boasts rich musical traditions with therapeutic uses.
  - ✓ Sufi Music: In Sufism, a mystical branch of Islam, music and dance (e.g., the whirling dervishes) are used to achieve spiritual ecstasy and divine connection. Sufi music, particularly the practice of

Qawwali, is believed to purify the soul and foster inner peace.

- ✓ Persian Classical Music: Persian traditional music has been used for therapeutic purposes for centuries. The modal systems, known as dastgahs, are thought to evoke specific emotional states, helping individuals to process and heal from emotional traumas.

- Western Perspectives: In the Western world, the scientific study of music therapy has gained prominence.
  - ✓ Modern Music Therapy: Rooted in the mid-20th century, modern music therapy involves structured interventions led by trained therapists. Techniques include playing instruments, songwriting, and guided listening, tailored to address various health conditions such as autism, depression, and chronic pain.
  - ✓ Neurological Music Therapy (NMT): This specialised branch of music therapy focuses on using rhythm and melody to retrain the brain in patients with neurological disorders like stroke, Parkinson's disease, and traumatic brain injuries.

Across the globe, music transcends cultural boundaries, serving as a universal language of healing and unity. Whether through ancient rituals or modern therapeutic practices, the harmonising power of music continues to be a vital tool in fostering health and well-being. By embracing these diverse cultural perspectives, we can deepen our understanding and appreciation of music's profound role in the healing process.

8.1. Music Therapy Traditions around the World

Music therapy, the clinical use of music to accomplish individualised goals, has roots in ancient traditions and practices across diverse cultures. This therapeutic approach leverages the emotional, cognitive, and social benefits of music to promote health and well-being. Let's explore how various cultures around the world have utilised music as a healing tool, contributing to the rich tapestry of music therapy traditions we see today.

- Africa: In many African cultures, music is an integral part of daily life and community well-being. Traditional African music therapy often involves drumming, chanting, and dancing. The drum, for instance, is not just an instrument but a conduit for spiritual connection and communication. Music is used in rituals to heal illnesses, invoke spirits, and bring about communal harmony. The Bantu people of Central Africa use specific rhythms and songs to facilitate healing and promote social cohesion.
- Indigenous Cultures of the Americas: Among Indigenous cultures in North and South America, music is deeply intertwined with spiritual and healing practices. Native American tribes use drumming, flutes, and chanting in their healing rituals. The sound of the drum is often believed to bridge the physical and spiritual realms, facilitating the healing process. In South America, the Quechua people incorporate music into their traditional medicine practices, utilising songs and instruments such as the pan flute to treat emotional and physical ailments.
- Asia: In Asia, music therapy has its roots in various cultural and spiritual practices that date back to ancient times. In China, traditional music therapy can be traced back to the times of Confucius, who emphasised the moral and healing power of music. Chinese music therapy often involves the use of traditional instruments, such as the guqin and the erhu, aiming to balance the body's energies and emotions according to the principles of yin and yang.

- India: In India, music therapy is closely tied to the ancient practice of Nada Yoga, which emphasises the spiritual and healing aspects of sound and music. Indian classical music, with its intricate ragas and rhythms, is used therapeutically to promote mental and emotional well-being. Specific ragas are believed to have distinct effects on the mind and body, aiding in relaxation, concentration, and emotional balance.
- Middle East: In the Middle East, music therapy has historical roots in the Sufi traditions of Islamic mysticism. Sufi music, characterised by devotional songs (Qawwali) and the rhythmic dance of the whirling dervishes, is used to induce spiritual states and facilitate healing. The therapeutic use of music in this context aims to connect the individual with the divine, promoting inner peace and emotional healing.
- Europe: Europe has a rich history of music therapy, with formalised practices emerging in the 20th century. However, traditional uses of music for healing can be traced back to ancient Greece, where philosophers like Pythagoras and Plato recognised the therapeutic potential of music. In medieval Europe, music was used in religious contexts to uplift the soul and provide comfort. Today, European music therapy is a well-established field that integrates scientific research with traditional practices to treat a wide range of psychological and physiological conditions.

Music therapy traditions around the world reflect the universal recognition of music's power to heal and transform. While the methods and instruments may vary, the underlying principle remains the same: music is a profound tool for enhancing health and well-being. By understanding and appreciating these diverse traditions, modern music therapy continues to evolve, drawing on ancient wisdom to address contemporary needs.

8.2. The Role of Music in Cultural Identity and Community

Music is a universal language that transcends boundaries and unites people across the globe. It is a powerful medium for expressing cultural identity and fostering a sense of community. From traditional folk songs to contemporary genres, music reflects the history, values, and experiences of different cultures, playing a vital role in shaping and preserving cultural identity.

8.2.1. Music as a Marker of Cultural Identity

Music is deeply embedded in cultural traditions and practices, serving as a key marker of cultural identity. It embodies the collective memory and experiences of a community, conveying stories, values, and beliefs that have been passed down through generations.

8.2.2. Traditional Folk Music

Traditional folk music is one of the most prominent examples of music's role in cultural identity. Each culture has its own unique folk music that captures the essence of its people's way of life. For instance, Irish folk music, with its distinct melodies and rhythms, reflects the history and spirit of the Irish people. Similarly, African American spirituals and blues music convey the struggles and resilience of African Americans throughout history.

8.2.3. National Anthems and Patriotic Songs

National anthems and patriotic songs are powerful symbols of national identity and unity. They evoke a sense of pride and belonging among citizens, reinforcing their connection to their homeland. The Star-Spangled Banner in the United States, La Marseillaise in France, and Jana Gana Mana in India are examples of how music serves to unify a nation and instil a sense of collective identity.

8.2.4. Music as a Tool for Community Building

Music is a powerful tool for building and strengthening communities. It brings people together, creating shared experiences and fostering a sense of belonging.

8.2.5. Festivals and Celebrations

Music plays a central role in festivals and celebrations, which are often key events in community life. These occasions provide an opportunity for people to come together, celebrate their cultural heritage, and strengthen their communal bonds. For example, Carnival in Brazil, Diwali in India, and the Day of the Dead in Mexico all feature music as a core component of their festivities, reflecting the cultural significance and communal spirit of these events.

8.2.6. Social Movements and Solidarity

Throughout history, music has been a vital tool in social movements, helping to unite people in the pursuit of common goals. Protest songs and anthems like "We Shall Overcome" during the Civil Rights Movement in the United States, "Nkosi Sikelel' iAfrika" during the anti-apartheid struggle in South Africa, and "Do You Hear the People Sing?" from the musical Les Misérables have inspired communities to fight for justice and equality. These songs foster a sense of solidarity and shared purpose among participants, strengthening their resolve and commitment to the cause.

8.2.7. Music and Cultural Exchange

Music also plays a significant role in cultural exchange, facilitating understanding and appreciation between different cultures. Through the global dissemination of music, people are exposed to diverse cultural expressions, fostering cross cultural dialogue and mutual respect.

8.2.8. World Music and Fusion Genres

The rise of world music and fusion genres illustrates how music can bridge cultural divides and create new forms of artistic expression. Artists like Ravi Shankar, who introduced Indian classical music to Western audiences, and bands like Buena Vista Social Club, which brought Cuban music to global prominence, have played a crucial role in promoting cultural exchange through music. Fusion genres, such as Afrobeat, which blends African rhythms with jazz and funk, and Reggaeton, which combines Latin American and Caribbean influences, demonstrate the creative possibilities that emerge from cross-cultural musical collaborations.

Music is a fundamental aspect of cultural identity and community. It reflects the values, history, and experiences of different cultures, serving as a marker of identity and a tool for community building. Through festivals, social movements, and cultural exchange, music unites people, fosters a sense of belonging, and promotes mutual understanding. In an increasingly interconnected world, the role of music in cultural identity and community remains as vital as ever, highlighting its enduring power to connect and inspire.

8.3. Comparative Case Studies: Cultural Perspectives on Music and Healing

Music has long been recognised for its therapeutic properties across various cultures. The ways in which music is utilised for healing differ greatly, reflecting distinct cultural perspectives and practices. This comparative study examines music and healing traditions across diverse cultural contexts, highlighting how music is utilised to foster physical, emotional, and spiritual well-being.

8.3.1. Case Study 1: Native American Healing Ceremonies

- Cultural Context: Native American cultures have a rich tradition of using music as a healing tool, deeply intertwined with their spiritual beliefs and practices. Music is considered a bridge between the physical and spiritual worlds, facilitating communication with ancestors and spirits.

- Healing Practices: In many Native American tribes, healing ceremonies often involve chanting, drumming, and the use of traditional instruments, such as flutes and rattles. The drum, often regarded as the heartbeat of Mother Earth, is central to these rituals. Healing ceremonies, such as the sweat lodge and the Sun Dance, incorporate music to induce trance-like states, promote spiritual cleansing, and restore balance to the individual's body and spirit.
- Impact and Significance: The repetitive rhythms and chants are believed to harmonise the mind and body, creating a meditative state that facilitates healing. Music in these ceremonies is not just an auditory experience but a holistic practice involving movement, symbolism, and community participation, emphasising the interconnectedness of all life.

8.3.2. Case Study 2: Gamelan Therapy in Bali, Indonesia

- Cultural Context: In Bali, Indonesia, the traditional ensemble music known as gamelan plays a significant role in social and religious life. Gamelan music, characterised by its intricate rhythms and melodies, is deeply embedded in Balinese culture.
- Healing Practices: Gamelan therapy is an emerging field that utilises the unique sounds and rhythms of gamelan music for therapeutic purposes. This practice involves group music-making sessions where participants play various instruments, such as metallophones, xylophones, and gongs. The collaborative nature of gamelan, where each

instrument contributes to the whole, reflects the communal values of Balinese society.

- Impact and Significance: Research has demonstrated that gamelan therapy can effectively reduce stress, enhance emotional well-being, and foster social cohesion. The immersive and participatory experience of playing gamelan helps individuals connect with their emotions and with others, fostering a sense of community and shared purpose. The music's complex interlocking rhythms also stimulate cognitive and motor functions, contributing to overall mental and physical health.

8.3.3. Case Study 3: Chinese Medicine and Music Therapy

- Cultural Context: Traditional Chinese medicine (TCM) views health as a state of balance between the body's energies, known as qi. Music has been used in TCM for thousands of years to harmonise these energies and promote healing.
- Healing Practices: Chinese music therapy often involves listening to or playing traditional instruments, such as the guqin (a seven-string plucked instrument) and the erhu (a two-string bowed instrument). Specific musical modes and scales, associated with different elements and organs in the body, are used to address various health issues. For example, the pentatonic scale is believed to correspond with the five elements (wood, fire, earth, metal, and water) and can be used to balance these energies.
- Impact and Significance: Music in TCM is used to regulate emotions, reduce stress, and restore physiological balance. The therapeutic process involves both passive listening and active participation, tailored to the individual's needs and the specific condition being treated. The integration of

music with other TCM practices, such as acupuncture and herbal medicine, underscores the holistic approach to health and well-being in Chinese culture.

8.3.4. Case Study 4: Music Therapy in Western Clinical Settings

- Cultural Context: In Western societies, music therapy is a well-established field that combines music with clinical practices to address a wide range of psychological and physiological conditions. This approach is rooted in scientific research and is practised by trained professionals.
- Healing Practices: Music therapy in Western settings often involves structured sessions where therapists use music-based interventions to achieve therapeutic goals. Techniques may include songwriting, improvisation, and guided imagery with music. Patients may listen to music, play instruments, or engage in vocal activities, depending on their needs and preferences.
- Impact and Significance: Numerous studies have demonstrated the effectiveness of music therapy in reducing symptoms of depression, anxiety, and pain, as well as improving cognitive and motor functions. In clinical settings, music therapy is used to support patients with conditions such as autism, dementia, and post-traumatic stress disorder (PTSD). The scientific approach to music therapy in the West emphasises evidence-based practices and measurable outcomes, providing a complementary method to traditional medical treatments.

These comparative case studies illustrate the diverse cultural perspectives on music and healing. While the methods and contexts vary, the underlying principle remains consistent: music is a powerful tool for enhancing health and well-being. By understanding and appreciating these different traditions, we can gain a deeper insight into the universal role of music in healing and explore new possibilities for integrating these practices into contemporary therapeutic approaches.

9 | Music in Everyday Mental Health

Music has long been recognised as a powerful tool for human expression and communication. It transcends language barriers and cultural differences, touching emotions and altering moods. In recent years, a growing body of research has highlighted the significant impact of music on mental health. Whether through passive listening, active participation, or therapeutic interventions, music plays a vital role in maintaining and improving mental well-being.

- The Science behind Music and Mental Health: Research in neuroscience and psychology has demonstrated that music can influence brain function and structure. Listening to music activates multiple areas of the brain, including those involved in emotion, memory, and motor control. These activations can lead to various mental health benefits:
  - ✓ Reduction of Stress and Anxiety: Music has been shown to lower levels of cortisol, a stress hormone, leading to reduced feelings of stress and anxiety. Calming music can slow the heart rate and breathing, promoting relaxation.
  - ✓ Mood Enhancement: Listening to upbeat or favourite music can increase the production of dopamine, a neurotransmitter associated with pleasure and reward. This can enhance mood and combat feelings of depression.
  - ✓ Cognitive Function: Music can improve focus, memory, and cognitive flexibility. It has been used in therapeutic settings to help patients with

neurological conditions such as Alzheimer's disease.

- Practical Applications of Music in Daily Life: Incorporating music into everyday life can be simple and effective. Here are some practical ways to use music for mental health:
- ✓ Morning Routine: Start the day with energising music to boost mood and motivation. Creating a playlist of favourite songs can help set a positive tone for the day.
- ✓ Work and Study: Instrumental or classical music can enhance concentration and productivity. It can be particularly beneficial in reducing distractions and improving focus.
- ✓ Exercise: Upbeat music can enhance physical performance and make exercise more enjoyable. It can serve as a great motivator during workouts.
- ✓ Relaxation and Sleep: Soft, calming music can be used during relaxation or bedtime routines to improve sleep quality. It helps unwind and prepare the mind for rest.
- ✓ Social Connection: Sharing music with friends or participating in group musical activities, such as singing in a choir or attending concerts, can foster social bonds and a sense of community.
- Music Therapy: Music therapy is a clinical and evidence-based use of music interventions to accomplish individualised goals within a therapeutic relationship. Conducted by a certified music therapist, it can address a wide range of mental health issues, including:
    - ✓ Depression and Anxiety: Structured music therapy sessions can help individuals express emotions, reduce anxiety, and improve mood.
    - ✓ Trauma and PTSD: Music therapy can provide a safe space for processing traumatic experiences and promoting healing.

- ✓ Developmental and Behavioural Disorders: For individuals with autism or ADHD, music therapy can enhance communication skills, social interaction, and behavioural regulation.

Music is a versatile and accessible tool for enhancing everyday mental health. Whether through listening to favourite tunes, engaging in musical activities, or seeking professional music therapy, the benefits of music are profound and far-reaching. By integrating music into daily routines, individuals can harness its power to improve mental well-being and overall quality of life.

9.1. Incorporating Music into Daily Life for Well-being

Music has an incredible ability to influence our emotions, thoughts, and overall well-being. Whether it is to lift our spirits, calm our minds, or motivate us, music can be a powerful tool in our daily lives. By intentionally incorporating music into our routines, we can enhance our mental, emotional, and even physical health.

<u>9.1.1. Starting the Day Right</u>

- Morning Playlist: Create a playlist of upbeat and positive songs to play in the morning. This can help set a positive tone for the day, increase energy levels, and improve mood.
- Mindful Morning Routine: Combine music with your morning routine. Play calming tunes while having breakfast, meditating, or stretching. This can make these activities more enjoyable and help reduce morning stress.

<u>9.1.2. Boosting Productivity and Focus</u>

- Work and Study: Use instrumental or classical music to enhance concentration and productivity during work or study sessions. Music without lyrics is often less distracting and can help maintain focus.

- Background Music: Light, ambient music can create a pleasant work environment and reduce background noise, which can help improve focus and efficiency.

9.1.3. Enhancing Physical Activity

- Exercise Motivation: Create a high-energy playlist for workouts. Upbeat music can increase motivation, improve physical performance, and make exercise more enjoyable.
- Rhythmic Activities: Use music with a strong beat to guide activities like running, cycling, or aerobics. The rhythm can help maintain a consistent pace, making the activity feel more natural and enjoyable.

9.1.4. Relaxation and Stress Relief

- Unwind After Work: Play soothing music in the evening to help transition from the stress of work to a more relaxed state. This can be especially effective during a commute home or while unwinding at home.
- Bedtime Routine: Incorporate calming music into your bedtime routine. Soft, slow-tempo music can help relax the mind and body, making it easier to fall asleep and improve sleep quality.

9.1.5. Social Connection and Enjoyment

- Shared Music Experiences: Share favourite songs and playlists with friends and family. Create communal playlists for gatherings or virtual hangouts to enhance social bonds.
- Live Music and Events: Attend live music events, concerts, or local performances. These experiences can foster a sense of community and provide a unique form of entertainment and enjoyment.

9.1.6. Personal Expression and Creativity

- Playing Instruments: Learn to play a musical instrument. This can be a fulfilling way to express creativity, reduce stress, and improve cognitive skills.
- Singing and Dancing: Engage in singing or dancing, whether alone or with others. These activities can boost your mood, increase energy levels, and provide a fun way to stay active.

9.1.7. Music Therapy

- Therapeutic Listening: Use specific types of music to address emotional and psychological needs. For instance, listening to music designed for relaxation or mindfulness can help manage anxiety and depression.
- Professional Guidance: Consider seeking music therapy from a certified music therapist if dealing with significant mental health issues. Music therapy can offer structured and evidence-based interventions to support mental health and well-being.

Incorporating music into daily life is a simple yet effective way to enhance well-being. Whether it is through listening to favourite songs, engaging in musical activities, or seeking professional music therapy, music offers a versatile tool for improving mental, emotional, and physical health. By incorporating music into your daily routine, you can harness its power to enrich your life and foster a greater sense of happiness and balance.

9.2. Building Playlists for Mood Management

Music has a profound impact on our emotions and can be a powerful tool for managing mood. By carefully selecting and organising songs into playlists, you can create a personalised soundtrack that supports your emotional well-being. Whether you want to boost your energy, relax, focus, or lift your spirits, building the right playlist can make a significant difference.

9.2.1. Steps to Build Effective Playlists

- Identify Your Mood Goals: Determine the specific mood or emotional state you want to achieve. Are you looking to energise yourself, relax, concentrate, or uplift your spirits? Knowing your goal will guide your song selection.
- Select Suitable Songs: Choose songs that match the mood you want to create. Consider the tempo, lyrics, and overall feel of the music. For example, upbeat songs with fast tempos are great for energising, while slower, soothing tracks are ideal for relaxation.
- Organise by Theme: Group songs by themes that resonate with your mood goals. You might have playlists for morning motivation, stress relief, deep focus, or happiness boosters.
- Mix Familiar and New: Combine familiar favourites with new discoveries. Familiar songs can provide comfort and nostalgia, while new tracks can add excitement and variety to your playlists.
- Consider the Flow: Arrange songs in a sequence that maintains the desired mood and flow. Start with songs that gently lead into the mood and build up to more intense tracks if needed. Ensure the transitions between songs are smooth to avoid jarring changes in tempo or style.

9.2.2. Playlist Ideas for Different Moods

- Energising Playlist
  - ✓ Purpose: To boost energy and motivation.
  - ✓ Features: Upbeat tempos, lively rhythms, and positive lyrics.
  - ✓ Examples: Pop, dance, rock, and upbeat electronic music.
- Suggested Tracks
  - ✓ "Happy" by Pharrell Williams

- ✓ "Uptown Funk" by Mark Ronson ft. Bruno Mars
- ✓ "Can't Stop the Feeling!" by Justin Timberlake

- Relaxation Playlist
  - ✓ Purpose: To unwind and reduce stress.
  - ✓ Features: Slow tempos, soft melodies, and calming sounds.
  - ✓ Examples: Ambient, classical, acoustic, and soft jazz music.
- Suggested Tracks
  - ✓ "Weightless" by Marconi Union
  - ✓ "Clair de Lune" by Claude Debussy
  - ✓ "Breathe Me" by Sia
- Focus Playlist
  - ✓ Purpose: To enhance concentration and productivity.
  - ✓ Features: Instrumental tracks, minimal lyrics, and steady rhythms.
  - ✓ Examples: Classical, lo-fi beats, instrumental hip-hop, and ambient music.
- Suggested Tracks
  - ✓ "Gymnopédie No. 1" by Erik Satie
  - ✓ "Time" by Hans Zimmer
  - ✓ "Lofi Hip Hop Radio" on YouTube
- Mood Boosting Playlist
  - ✓ Purpose: To elevate mood and combat feelings of sadness.
  - ✓ Features: Positive lyrics, upbeat tempos, and catchy melodies.
  - ✓ Examples: Pop, indie, upbeat rock, and feel-good anthems.
- Suggested Tracks:
  - ✓ "Walking on Sunshine" by Katrina and the Waves
  - ✓ "Good as Hell" by Lizzo
  - ✓ "Best Day of My Life" by American Authors
- Sleep Playlist

- ✓ Purpose: To promote relaxation and better sleep.
- ✓ Features: Soft, slow-tempo music with gentle rhythms.
- ✓ Examples: Ambient, classical, and nature sounds.

- Suggested Tracks
  - ✓ "Moonlight Sonata" by Ludwig van Beethoven
  - ✓ "Canon in D" by Johann Pachelbel
  - ✓ "Healing Waters" by Dean Evenson

9.2.3. Tips for Personalising Your Playlists

- Listen to Your Body: Pay attention to how different songs make you feel and adjust your playlist accordingly. Everyone responds differently to music, so personalise your choices to fit your unique preferences.
- Update Regularly: Refresh your playlists periodically to keep them interesting and relevant. Adding new songs and removing those that no longer resonate can help maintain the desired mood.
- Use Streaming Services: Take advantage of streaming platforms like Spotify, Apple Music, or YouTube, which offer curated playlists and personalised recommendations based on your listening habits.
- Experiment with Genres: Do not be afraid to explore different genres and styles of music. Sometimes, unexpected choices can have a surprising impact on your mood.

Building playlists for mood management is a powerful and enjoyable way to enhance your emotional well-being. By thoughtfully selecting and organising music, you can create soundtracks that support your daily activities and help you navigate life's emotional ups and downs. Whether you need a pick-me-up, a moment of calm, or a boost in focus, the right playlist can make all the difference.

9.3. Music and Social Connections

Music is more than just an art form; it is a universal language that brings people together. Throughout history, music has played a pivotal role in fostering social connections, building communities, and strengthening bonds between individuals. From communal singing and dancing to modern online music communities, music creates shared experiences that bridge cultural and social gaps.

9.3.1. The Role of Music in Social Connection

- Cultural Expression: Music is a vital part of cultural identity. It carries traditions, stories, and values from one generation to the next. Participating in cultural music events helps individuals feel a sense of belonging and pride in their heritage.
- Shared Experiences: Music events such as concerts, festivals, and dance parties provide opportunities for people to gather and share collective experiences. These events foster a sense of unity and camaraderie among attendees, creating lasting memories and friendships.
- Emotional Bonding: Listening to music together can deepen emotional bonds. Whether it is a romantic couple sharing a favourite song, friends attending a concert, or a family singing together, music can enhance intimacy and connection.
- Social Movements: Music has historically been a powerful tool for social change. Protest songs and anthems rally people around a cause, unify voices, and inspire action. From civil rights movements to environmental activism, music has driven collective efforts toward social justice.

9.3.2. Ways Music Fosters Social Connections

- Group Activities: Singing and Choirs: Participating in a choir or singing group offers a sense of community and shared purpose. The act of harmonising and creating music together builds trust and cooperation.
- Dance Classes: Group dance activities, such as salsa, ballroom, or line dancing, offer social interaction and physical exercise. These classes often foster friendships and a sense of community.
- Music Festivals and Concerts: Attending live music events is a communal activity that brings people from diverse backgrounds together. The shared enjoyment of music in a live setting creates a unique and powerful bond among attendees.
- Music and Technology: Online Communities: Digital platforms like Spotify, SoundCloud, and YouTube create virtual spaces where music lovers can share playlists, discover new artists, and discuss their favourite tracks. Social media groups and forums dedicated to specific genres or artists also foster connections among fans.
- Collaborative Playlists: Platforms that allow multiple users to contribute to a playlist encourage collaboration and sharing. Friends, family, or co-workers can create and enjoy a shared soundtrack, enhancing their social bonds.
- Intergenerational Connections: Music often serves as a bridge between generations. Grandparents sharing old records with grandchildren or parents teaching their kids to play an instrument can create meaningful connections across age groups.

9.3.3. Music Therapy and Social Connections

Music therapy not only addresses individual health but also promotes social interactions. Group music therapy sessions, such as drumming circles or music-making workshops, can help individuals develop social skills, build relationships, and foster a sense of community.

- Community Building: Music therapy programs in schools, hospitals, and community centres can create supportive environments where individuals feel connected and understood.
- Improving Communication: For individuals with communication difficulties, such as those with autism or speech disorders, music therapy can enhance social interaction and expressive abilities, leading to improved relationships with peers and family members.

Music is a powerful connector that transcends language and cultural barriers, uniting people in diverse social contexts. Whether through live events, shared listening experiences, or digital platforms, music creates opportunities for meaningful connections and community building. By embracing the social aspects of music, individuals can enrich their lives, strengthen their relationships, and foster a greater sense of belonging and unity.

10| Music, Media, and Mental Health

In today's digital age, the intersection of music, media, and mental health has become increasingly prominent. Music, delivered through various media channels, can profoundly impact mental well-being. From streaming platforms and social media to television and movies, music is a constant presence in our lives, providing a versatile tool for managing emotions, relieving stress, and promoting overall mental well-being.

- The Impact of Music on Mental Health
  - ✓ Emotional Regulation: Music has the power to evoke a wide range of emotions. Listening to music that resonates with our current mood can help process and regulate emotions, providing an outlet for expression and understanding.
  - ✓ Stress Reduction: Calming music, such as classical or ambient genres, can reduce stress and anxiety levels by lowering cortisol, the stress hormone. This effect can lead to improved relaxation and mental clarity.
  - ✓ Mood Enhancement: Upbeat and positive music can boost mood and increase feelings of happiness. Music with a fast tempo and a major key can elevate energy levels and combat feelings of depression.
  - ✓ Cognitive Benefits: Music can enhance cognitive functions such as memory, attention, and problem-solving skills. Background music, particularly instrumental tracks, can improve focus and productivity during tasks.
- Music in Media and Its Influence

- ✓ Streaming Platforms: Platforms like Spotify, Apple Music, and YouTube Music offer vast libraries of songs and playlists tailored to various moods and activities. Personalised recommendations and curated playlists make it easy for users to find music that supports their mental health needs.
- ✓ Social Media: Social media platforms enable users to share their musical tastes and discover new music through friends, influencers, and trends. Hashtags and communities centred around mental health and music, such as #MusicTherapy or #MentalHealthAwareness, provide support and resources for individuals seeking emotional relief through music.
- ✓ Television and Film: Soundtracks and scores in TV shows and movies play a crucial role in setting the emotional tone and enhancing storytelling. Music can amplify the emotional impact of scenes, helping viewers connect with characters and narratives on a deeper level. This emotional engagement can provide catharsis and a sense of shared experience.
- ✓ Podcasts and Radio: Music-focused podcasts and radio shows offer discussions on the therapeutic benefits of music, interviews with musicians, and curated playlists that support mental health. These media formats provide educational content and inspiration, enabling listeners to explore the connection between music and well-being.

- The Role of Music Therapy in Media
  - ✓ Awareness and Advocacy: Documentaries and TV programs that highlight music therapy bring awareness to its benefits for mental health. These media portrayals can destigmatise mental health

issues and encourage individuals to seek music therapy as a viable treatment option.

- ✓ Educational Content: Online courses, webinars, and YouTube channels dedicated to music therapy educate the public on techniques and practices for using music to improve mental health. This accessible content empowers individuals to incorporate music therapy principles into their daily lives.

- Practical Tips for Using Music and Media for Mental Health
  - ✓ Curate Personal Playlists: Create playlists tailored to different emotional states or activities. For example, create a playlist for relaxation, another for motivation, and a third for mood-lifting. Personalising these playlists ensures that the music you listen to aligns with your mental health goals.
  - ✓ Engage with Music Communities: Join online communities and social media groups focused on music and mental health. Sharing experiences and discovering new music within these communities can provide support and connection.
  - ✓ Mindful Listening: Practise mindful listening by fully immersing yourself in the music. Focus on the melodies, lyrics, and emotions evoked by the music. This practice can enhance the therapeutic effects of music and improve emotional awareness.
  - ✓ Explore Music Therapy Resources: Utilise resources such as music therapy apps, podcasts, and educational videos to learn more about how music can support mental health. Implementing

music therapy techniques in daily routines can enhance mental well-being.

The convergence of music, media, and mental health offers a powerful toolkit for emotional regulation, stress relief, and cognitive enhancement. By leveraging the accessibility of music through various media channels, individuals can harness its therapeutic potential to improve their mental well-being. Whether through curated playlists, engaging with music communities, or exploring music therapy resources, music remains a vital and effective component of mental health care in the digital age.

10.1. The Impact of Music in Media on Mental Health

Music is a ubiquitous part of media, permeating movies, television shows, video games, and advertisements. Its powerful influence on emotions and cognition makes it a significant factor in shaping our mental health. Understanding the impact of music in media on mental well-being can help individuals harness its benefits and mitigate potential negative effects.

- Emotional Resonance and Psychological Effects

✓ Mood Enhancement: Music in media can instantly elevate mood. Upbeat soundtracks and positive songs can infuse a sense of joy and excitement. For instance, a lively song in a commercial or a high-energy track in a video game can boost the spirits of viewers or players.

✓ Stress Reduction: Calming and soothing music in films or TV shows can reduce stress and anxiety. Background scores with slow tempos and mellow tones promote relaxation, helping viewers unwind.

✓ Emotional Catharsis: Music can amplify emotional experiences in media, providing catharsis. A poignant song during a movie's climax can evoke tears and facilitate the release of pent-up emotions, thereby contributing to emotional processing and healing.

- Music in Movies and Television
  - ✓ Storytelling and Character Development: Music enhances storytelling by conveying the emotional undertones of scenes and providing insight into characters' inner worlds. This emotional depth enables viewers to connect with the story and characters, fostering empathy and a deeper understanding.
  - ✓ Memorable Moments: Iconic music moments in films and TV shows create lasting memories and cultural touchstones. These moments can bring comfort and nostalgia, positively impacting mental health by evoking pleasant memories.
  - ✓ Soundtrack as a Coping Mechanism: Many people use movie and TV show soundtracks as a coping mechanism during tough times. Listening to familiar soundtracks can provide a sense of stability and comfort, helping to manage anxiety and depression.
- Music in Video Games
  - ✓ Immersive Experience: Music in video games enhances the immersive experience, drawing players into the game world. Engaging soundtracks and sound effects contribute to a sense of presence and escape, which can be therapeutic for stress relief and overall well-being.
  - ✓ Motivation and Achievement: Upbeat and motivating music in games can boost players' motivation and sense of achievement. This positive reinforcement can improve mood and encourage perseverance, translating to real-life resilience.

- ✓ Community and Social Interaction: Multiplayer games often have iconic soundtracks that foster a sense of community among players. Shared musical experiences in games can strengthen social bonds and provide a sense of belonging.

- Potential Negative Impacts
  - ✓ Overstimulation: Intense or loud music in media can lead to overstimulation and increased stress levels. Fast-paced, high-volume music, especially in action sequences or advertisements, can elevate heart rates and create anxiety.
  - ✓ Negative Emotional Triggers: Music associated with negative or traumatic scenes can act as emotional triggers. Hearing certain songs might bring back distressing memories or amplify negative emotions, impacting mental well-being.
  - ✓ Desensitisation: Constant exposure to certain types of music, particularly those with aggressive or violent themes, can lead to desensitisation. This can affect emotional regulation and empathy, potentially leading to negative behavioural changes.
- Practical Tips for Harnessing the Benefits
  - ✓ Curated Playlists: Create playlists of positive and calming music from favourite movies, TV shows, or games to use as a mood booster or relaxation tool. Tailor these playlists to specific needs, such as stress relief or motivation.
  - ✓ Mindful Consumption: Be mindful of the types of media consumed and their musical content. Opt for media with music that promotes positive emotions and avoids overstimulation or negative triggers.

- Engage with Soundtracks
    - ✓ Explore the Soundtracks of Beloved Media: Actively listening to and engaging with these soundtracks can provide comfort and emotional support, especially during challenging times.
    - ✓ Community Interaction: Join online communities or forums that discuss favourite media soundtracks. Sharing experiences and discovering new music through these communities can offer social support and improve overall well-being.

The integration of music in media has a profound impact on mental health, offering both benefits and challenges. By leveraging the positive aspects, such as emotional enhancement, stress reduction, and social connection, and being mindful of potential negative effects, individuals can use music in media to support their mental well-being. Whether through movies, TV shows, video games, or advertisements, music remains a powerful tool in shaping our emotional landscapes and enhancing our quality of life.

10.2. Music in Advertising, Films, and Video Games

Music is an integral part of advertising, films, and video games. Its ability to evoke emotions, set the tone, and enhance storytelling makes it a powerful tool across these media. Understanding how music is used in these contexts can provide insights into its impact on audiences and its role in creating memorable experiences.

- Music in Advertising
    - ✓ Emotional Appeal: Music in advertising plays a crucial role in creating an emotional connection with the audience. A well-chosen song can evoke feelings of happiness, nostalgia, or excitement, making the ad more memorable and impactful.
    - ✓ Brand Identity: Companies use specific music styles or jingles to establish their brand identity. A

consistent musical theme helps reinforce brand recognition and loyalty. Iconic jingles, such as McDonald's "I'm Lovin' It" or Intel's sound logo, are instantly recognisable and associated with their respective brands.

- ✓ Target Audience: Advertisers select music that resonates with their target audience. For instance, ads targeting younger demographics might feature contemporary pop or hip-hop, while those aimed at older audiences might use classic rock or jazz.
- ✓ Setting the Tone: Music helps set the tone and mood of an advertisement. Upbeat, fast-paced music can create a sense of excitement and urgency, while slower, more melodic tunes can evoke a sense of relaxation and comfort.

- Music in Films
    - ✓ Emotional Depth: Music in films adds emotional depth to scenes, enhancing the audience's connection to the story and characters. It can underscore the emotional stakes, heightening joy, sadness, tension, or suspense.
    - ✓ Character and Theme: Film scores often include leitmotifs, or recurring musical themes associated with specific characters, locations, or ideas. This technique helps reinforce narrative elements and deepen the audience's understanding of the story.
    - ✓ Atmosphere and Setting: Music sets the atmosphere and helps establish the setting of a film. For example, a historical drama might use period-specific instruments and compositions to transport the audience to a different time.
    - ✓ Iconic Moments: Many films have iconic musical moments that become ingrained in popular culture. The suspenseful notes of "Jaws," the

triumphant march of "Star Wars," or the emotional piano theme in "Titanic" are examples of how music can define a film's identity and legacy.

- Music in Video Games

✓ Immersive Experience: Music in video games enhances the immersive experience by drawing players into the game world. Dynamic soundtracks that adapt to in-game actions and environments help create a more engaging and interactive experience.

✓ Emotional Engagement: Just like in films, music in video games is used to evoke emotions. Whether it is the adrenaline-pumping tracks in action sequences or the soothing melodies in exploration scenes, music helps players connect emotionally with the game.

✓ Gameplay Enhancement: Music can influence gameplay by providing auditory cues and feedback. For example, a change in music tempo might indicate an approaching enemy or a time-sensitive challenge, enabling players to react and make informed decisions.

✓ Memorable Themes: Many video games have memorable themes that become iconic within the gaming community. The main theme from "The Legend of Zelda," the haunting melodies of "Silent Hill," or the epic orchestration of "Final Fantasy" are examples of how music can leave a lasting impression on players.

Music is a powerful tool in advertising, films, and video games, significantly impacting how these media are perceived and experienced. By evoking emotions, enhancing storytelling, and creating memorable moments, music plays a critical role in engaging audiences and leaving a lasting impression. Understanding its use in these contexts can deepen our appreciation for the artistry behind these media and the profound effect music has on our sensory and emotional experiences.

10.3. Ethical Considerations in Relation to Music in Advertising, Films, and Video Games

Music is a powerful tool used in advertising, films, and video games to influence emotions and behaviours. However, its usage raises several ethical considerations. These concerns revolve around issues like emotional manipulation, cultural appropriation, copyright infringement, and the impact on vulnerable populations. Understanding these ethical dimensions is crucial for both creators and consumers.

<u>10.3.1. Ethical Considerations in Music for Advertising</u>

- Emotional Manipulation
    - ✓ Concern: Music in advertising is often used to evoke specific emotions and drive consumer behaviour. This can be seen as manipulative, especially if it leads people to make decisions based on emotional responses rather than rational judgement.
    - ✓ Example: An advertisement using sentimental music to persuade viewers to donate to a cause or buy a product they do not need.
- Truth in Advertising:
    - ✓ Concern: The use of music can create a misleading representation of a product or service. Music might evoke feelings of trust or reliability that the product does not inherently possess.
    - ✓ Example: Using upbeat and happy music to sell a product that may not deliver the promised benefits.

- Targeting Vulnerable Populations
  - ✓ Concern: Advertisers often use music to target vulnerable populations, such as children or individuals with emotional vulnerabilities. This practice can be considered exploitative.
  - ✓ Example: Using catchy jingles to target children in fast food advertisements, encouraging unhealthy eating habits.

<u>10.3.2. Ethical Considerations in Music for Films</u>

- Cultural Appropriation
  - ✓ Concern: The use of music from different cultures without proper understanding, respect, or attribution can lead to cultural appropriation. This is particularly problematic when it perpetuates stereotypes or misrepresents cultural traditions.
  - ✓ Example: A film using traditional Native American music in a context that misrepresents or trivialises Native American culture.
- Representation and Stereotyping
  - ✓ Concern: Music can reinforce stereotypes and biased representations. Filmmakers must be careful about how musical choices might perpetuate harmful narratives.
  - ✓ Example: Using specific musical themes to signify "evil" characters based on cultural stereotypes.
- Emotional Impact
  - ✓ Concern: Films often use music to heighten emotional responses, which can be seen as manipulative. Filmmakers have a responsibility to use this power ethically, ensuring that it enhances the narrative without unduly influencing the audience's emotions.

- ✓ Example: Overly dramatic music in scenes of violence or trauma, which can be distressing or manipulative.

10.3.3. Ethical Considerations in Music for Video Games

- Addiction and Overstimulation
  - ✓ Concern: Video games often use music to create highly engaging experiences, which can contribute to addiction and overstimulation. Game designers must consider the potential impact on players' mental health.
  - ✓ Example: Intense, repetitive music that keeps players engaged for long periods, potentially leading to unhealthy gaming habits.
- Cultural Sensitivity
  - ✓ Concern: Like films, video games must handle cultural music with sensitivity. Misuse or inappropriate representation can lead to cultural insensitivity and offence.
  - ✓ Example: Incorporating traditional music from a culture without proper context or respect, leading to misrepresentation.
- Content Appropriateness:
  - ✓ Concern: The music in video games should be appropriate for the target audience. Games marketed to children should not include music with explicit or violent themes.
  - ✓ Example: A game rated for teens featuring music with adult content or themes that are not suitable for younger players.

10.3.4. Legal and Copyright Issues

- Copyright Infringement:
  - ✓ Concern: Unauthorised use of music can lead to legal issues and ethical concerns regarding

intellectual property rights. Creators must ensure they have the right to use the music included in their media.
    - ✓ Example: Using a popular song in an advertisement without securing the proper licences from the rights holders.
- Fair Compensation
    - ✓ Concern: Musicians and composers should be fairly compensated for their work. This includes not only financial payment but also proper credit and recognition.
    - ✓ Example: A film using a composer's work without proper credit or appropriate royalties.

Ethical considerations in the use of music in advertising, films, and video games are multifaceted, encompassing emotional manipulation, cultural sensitivity, and legal rights. By addressing these concerns, creators can use music responsibly, ensuring it enhances the audience's experience without causing harm or perpetuating injustice. Ethical practices in music usage not only protect the rights of musicians and composers but also foster a more respectful and inclusive media landscape.

11 | Creating Therapeutic Music Programs

Therapeutic music programs harness the power of music to promote healing, enhance well-being, and improve the quality of life for individuals facing physical, emotional, or psychological challenges. These programs can be implemented in various settings, including hospitals, schools, community centres, and mental health facilities. Designing an effective therapeutic music program requires a thoughtful approach, considering the specific needs of participants and the evidence-based practices that can achieve desired outcomes.

11.1. Key Components of Therapeutic Music Programs

- Assessment and Goal-Setting
  - ✓ Initial Assessment: Begin by evaluating the individual or group's needs, preferences, and current state of health. This assessment helps tailor the program to meet specific therapeutic goals.
  - ✓ Setting Goals: Define clear, achievable objectives for the program. Goals can range from reducing anxiety and stress to improving motor skills or fostering social interaction.
- Program Design
  - ✓ Personalisation: Customise the program to the preferences and needs of the participants. Consider factors such as age, cultural background, musical tastes, and the specific challenges they are facing.

- ✓ Variety of Activities: Incorporate a range of musical activities, including listening sessions, singing, playing instruments, songwriting, and movement to music. This variety can address different therapeutic goals and keep participants engaged.

- Qualified Facilitators:
  - ✓ Trained Professionals: Ensure that the program is led by certified music therapists or professionals with relevant training and experience. They should have the skills to adapt the program as needed and respond to participants' reactions.
  - ✓ Ongoing Training: Provide continuous education and training for facilitators to keep them updated on the latest research and techniques in music therapy.
- Evidence-Based Practices:
  - ✓ Research Integration: Base the program on established music therapy techniques and evidence-based practices. Use research to inform the choice of activities and interventions.
  - ✓ Monitoring and Evaluation: Regularly assess the effectiveness of the program through feedback, observations, and standardised measures. Use this data to make necessary adjustments and improve outcomes.

11.2. Types of Therapeutic Music Programs

- Music Therapy for Mental Health:
  - ✓ Target Audience: Individuals dealing with depression, anxiety, PTSD, or other mental health issues.
  - ✓ Activities: Guided imagery with music, songwriting, and improvisation. Focus on

expression, emotional release, and coping strategies.

- Music Therapy in Medical Settings:
  - ✓ Target Audience: Patients undergoing medical treatment, including those in hospitals, rehabilitation centres, and palliative care.
  - ✓ Activities: Live music performances at bedside, music-assisted relaxation techniques, and rhythmic auditory stimulation for motor rehabilitation.
- Music Therapy for Developmental Disorders:
  - ✓ Target Audience: Children and adults with autism, ADHD, or other developmental disorders.
  - ✓ Activities: Interactive musical games, structured music sessions to improve social skills, and rhythmic exercises to enhance attention and coordination.
- Community Music Programs:
  - ✓ Target Audience: General community members, including seniors, veterans, and at-risk youth.
  - ✓ Activities: Group singing, drumming circles, and community choir projects aimed at building social connections and fostering a sense of belonging.

11.3. Implementation Steps

- Planning and Coordination:
  - ✓ Needs Assessment: Conduct surveys or interviews to understand the community's needs and interests.
  - ✓ Resource Allocation: Secure funding, instruments, and space for the program. Partner with local organisations and stakeholders to support the initiative.
- Program Launch

  - ✓ Promotion: Advertise the program through local media, social networks, and community bulletin boards.
  - ✓ Initial Sessions: Start with pilot sessions to gather initial feedback and make any necessary adjustments before fully launching the program.
- Sustaining the Program:
  - ✓ Regular Feedback: Continuously collect feedback from participants and facilitators to refine and enhance the program.
  - ✓ Community Engagement: Involve the community through performances, showcases, and open sessions to build support and maintain interest.

11.4. Ethical Considerations

- Informed Consent
  - ✓ Ensure participants are fully informed about the program and its goals. Obtain consent, especially when working with vulnerable populations.
- Confidentiality
  - ✓ Maintain the confidentiality of participants' personal information and their experiences within the program.
- Cultural Sensitivity:
  - ✓ Respect and incorporate participants' cultural backgrounds and musical preferences. Avoid cultural appropriation and ensure inclusivity.
- Professional Boundaries
  - ✓ Facilitators should maintain professional boundaries and avoid dual relationships with participants to ensure a therapeutic environment.

Creating effective therapeutic music programs involves careful planning, skilled facilitation, and a commitment to evidence-based practices. By tailoring programs to meet specific needs and continuously evaluating their impact, music therapists and program designers can harness the therapeutic power of music to enhance mental, emotional, and physical well-being. Ethical considerations and cultural sensitivity are paramount in ensuring these programs are inclusive, respectful, and effective.

11.5. Designing Programs for Schools, Workplaces, and Communities

Music programs can have profound benefits across various settings, including schools, workplaces, and communities. These programs foster creativity, enhance well-being, and build stronger social bonds. Designing effective music programs tailored to the unique needs of each setting involves understanding the specific goals, challenges, and preferences of the participants.

11.5.1. Music Programs for Schools

- Objectives
  - ✓ Enhance cognitive development and academic performance.
  - ✓ Foster emotional expression and social skills.
  - ✓ Encourage creativity and cultural appreciation.
- Program Components:
  - ✓ General Music Education: Classes that introduce students to the basics of music theory, history, and practice. Activities include singing, playing instruments, and listening to a diverse range of musical genres.
  - ✓ Performance Ensembles: School bands, choirs, and orchestras that provide opportunities for group performance and individual musical growth.
  - ✓ Music Therapy Sessions: Targeted programs for students with special needs, using music to improve social, emotional, and motor skills.
- Implementation Steps

- ✓ Needs Assessment: Survey students, teachers, and parents to determine interests and needs.
- ✓ Curriculum Design: Develop a curriculum that aligns with educational standards and caters to different age groups and skill levels.
- ✓ Resource Allocation: Secure funding for instruments, sheet music, and qualified instructors. Partner with local musicians and music organisations for support.
- ✓ Regular Evaluation: Collect feedback from students and teachers to refine and improve the program.

- Benefits
  - ✓ Improved academic performance through enhanced memory and concentration.
  - ✓ Development of social skills and emotional intelligence.
  - ✓ Increased cultural awareness and appreciation for diversity.

11.5.2. Music Programs for Workplaces

- Objectives
  - ✓ Reduce stress and improve mental well-being.
  - ✓ Foster teamwork and enhance workplace culture.
  - ✓ Boost creativity and productivity.
- Program Components
  - ✓ Wellness Workshops: Sessions that use music for relaxation and stress relief, such as guided music meditation and rhythmic breathing exercises.
  - ✓ Team-Building Activities: Group drumming circles, corporate choirs, and collaborative music-making events to build camaraderie and teamwork.

- ✓ Background Music: Carefully curated playlists for different office environments to enhance focus, creativity, and relaxation.

- Implementation Steps
  - ✓ Employee Surveys: Gauge interest and identify specific needs and preferences.
  - ✓ Program Design: Develop a schedule of activities that fits into the workday without disrupting productivity.
  - ✓ Qualified Facilitators: Hire experienced music therapists or musicians to lead sessions.
  - ✓ Feedback Mechanism: Regularly collect feedback from employees to adapt and improve the program.
- Benefits
  - ✓ Reduced workplace stress and anxiety.
  - ✓ Enhanced team cohesion and communication.
  - ✓ Increased creativity and overall job satisfaction.

11.5.3. Music Programs for Communities

- Objectives
  - ✓ Build social connections and community spirit.
  - ✓ Provide accessible cultural and artistic experiences.
  - ✓ Support mental and emotional well-being.
- Program Components
  - ✓ Community Choirs and Bands: Open to all community members, offering regular rehearsals and performances to bring people together.
  - ✓ Music Workshops and Classes: Diverse offerings such as instrument lessons, songwriting workshops, and dance classes catering to different age groups and interests.

  - ✓ Public Performances and Events: Organising concerts, festivals, and open mic nights to showcase local talent and foster community pride.
- Implementation Steps
  - ✓ Community Outreach: Engage with local residents through surveys and public meetings to understand their interests and needs.
  - ✓ Partnerships: Collaborate with local schools, arts organisations, and businesses to pool resources and expertise.
  - ✓ Inclusive Programming: Ensure programs are accessible to all, including marginalised and underserved populations. Provide sliding scale fees or free participation options when possible.
  - ✓ Continuous Improvement: Gather feedback from participants and community leaders to continually refine and expand the program.
- Benefits
  - ✓ Strengthened community bonds and increased social capital.
  - ✓ Enhanced cultural vitality and local pride.
  - ✓ Improved mental health and well-being for community members.

11.5.4. Ethical Considerations

- Inclusivity and Accessibility
  - ✓ Ensure programs are inclusive, respecting diverse backgrounds and abilities. Provide accommodations for those with disabilities and consider socio-economic barriers.
- Cultural Sensitivity
  - ✓ Respect and celebrate cultural diversity in music selections and activities. Avoid cultural appropriation and strive for genuine representation and appreciation.

- Confidentiality and Consent
  - ✓ Maintain confidentiality of participants' information and obtain informed consent, especially in therapeutic settings.
- Professional Integrity
  - ✓ Ensure facilitators are qualified and adhere to ethical standards in their practice.

Designing music programs for schools, workplaces, and communities involves a tailored approach to meet specific goals and address unique challenges. By focusing on inclusivity, cultural sensitivity, and continuous improvement, these programs can foster creativity, enhance overall well-being, and strengthen social bonds. Whether improving academic performance in schools, reducing stress in the workplace, or strengthening community ties, music programs have the potential to make a significant, positive impact.

11.6. Implementing Music Interventions in Various Settings

Music interventions utilise the therapeutic properties of music to promote healing, enhance well-being, and achieve specific goals in various settings. Whether in healthcare, education, community outreach, or corporate environments, implementing effective music interventions requires thoughtful planning, qualified personnel, and consideration of the unique needs of participants.

11.6.1. Healthcare Settings

- Objectives
  - ✓ Pain Management: Use music to reduce pain perception and promote relaxation.
  - ✓ Emotional Support: Provide comfort and emotional expression for patients and families facing illness or end-of-life care.

  - ✓ Physical Rehabilitation: Utilise rhythmic auditory stimulation to improve motor coordination and movement.
- Program Components
  - ✓ Music Therapy Sessions: Led by certified music therapists, these sessions may include live music, guided imagery, and songwriting to address emotional, cognitive, and physical needs.
  - ✓ Music-Assisted Relaxation: Recorded music playlists designed to reduce stress and anxiety in waiting rooms, patient rooms, and treatment areas.
  - ✓ Patient Participation: Encourage patients to engage through music-making activities like drum circles or singing groups.
- Implementation Steps
  - ✓ Needs Assessment: Collaborate with healthcare professionals to identify patient needs and therapeutic goals.
  - ✓ Training and Certification: Ensure music therapists are trained and certified to provide safe and effective interventions.
  - ✓ Evaluation and Feedback: Regularly assess patient outcomes and satisfaction through surveys and feedback from healthcare staff.
  - ✓ Integration into Care Plans: Coordinate music interventions with medical treatments and rehabilitation programs to optimise patient care.

11.6.2. Educational Settings

- Objectives
  - ✓ Academic Enhancement: Improve cognitive skills, memory retention, and academic performance through music education.

- ✓ Social and Emotional Development: Foster creativity, communication, and teamwork skills among students.
- ✓ Behavioural Support: Use music to manage behaviour and promote positive learning environments.

- Program Components
  - ✓ General Music Education: Incorporate music classes, choirs, and instrumental ensembles into the school curriculum.
  - ✓ Music Therapy for Special Needs: Provide individual or group sessions for students with disabilities or behavioural challenges.
  - ✓ Performance Opportunities: Organise concerts, recitals, and music festivals to showcase student talent and build confidence.
- Implementation Steps
  - ✓ Curriculum Integration: Collaborate with educators to integrate music into core subjects and extracurricular activities.
  - ✓ Resource Allocation: Secure funding for instruments, sheet music, and qualified music instructors.
  - ✓ Parent and Community Engagement: Involve parents and community members in supporting music education through volunteerism and fundraising.
  - ✓ Assessment and Progress Monitoring: Use standardised assessments and teacher observations to measure academic and social-emotional progress.

11.6.3. Community Outreach Settings

- Objectives
  - ✓ Social Inclusion: Engage diverse community members through accessible and inclusive music programs.
  - ✓ Cultural Enrichment: Celebrate and preserve cultural heritage through music workshops, concerts, and festivals.
  - ✓ Health and Well-being: Improve mental health and quality of life through recreational music activities.
- Program Components:
  - ✓ Community Choirs and Bands: Offer open rehearsals and performances for participants of all ages and skill levels.
  - ✓ Music Workshops: Provide hands-on experiences in songwriting, music production, and dance.
  - ✓ Music Therapy for Vulnerable Populations: Implement targeted interventions for at-risk youth, seniors, and individuals experiencing homelessness or trauma.
- Implementation Steps
  - ✓ Community Needs Assessment: Conduct surveys and focus groups to understand local interests and barriers to participation.
  - ✓ Collaborative Partnerships: Forge alliances with local arts organisations, schools, and social service agencies to expand program reach and resources.
  - ✓ Accessibility and Inclusivity: Ensure programs are accessible to diverse populations by offering flexible scheduling, language support, and financial assistance.
  - ✓ Impact Evaluation: Measure outcomes such as social connectedness, cultural awareness, and individual well-being through participant surveys and program evaluations.

11.6.4. Corporate Settings

- Objectives
  - ✓ Employee Well-being: Use music to reduce workplace stress, enhance mood, and improve overall job satisfaction.
  - ✓ Team Building: Foster collaboration, communication, and morale among employees through musical activities.
  - ✓ Creativity and Innovation: Stimulate creativity and problem-solving skills through music-inspired workshops and events.
- Program Components
  - ✓ Music-Based Wellness Programs: Offer mindfulness sessions with music, relaxation playlists, and office background music.
  - ✓ Team-Building Activities: Conduct group drumming sessions, choir rehearsals, and collaborative songwriting workshops.
  - ✓ Live Performances and Events: Organise concerts, music-themed social gatherings, and musical competitions for employees.
- Implementation Steps
  - ✓ Leadership Support: Gain buy-in from corporate leadership by demonstrating the benefits of music interventions for employee engagement and productivity.
  - ✓ Employee Engagement: Solicit input from employees through focus groups or surveys to gauge interest and preferences.
  - ✓ Professional Facilitation: Hire experienced music facilitators or therapists to lead sessions and ensure a positive and inclusive experience.
  - ✓ Measurement of Impact: Track metrics such as employee satisfaction, stress levels, and teamwork

effectiveness to assess program success and make improvements.

11.6.5. Ethical Considerations

- Informed Consent: Obtain consent from participants, especially in therapeutic settings, and respect their right to privacy and confidentiality.
- Cultural Sensitivity: Acknowledge and respect diverse cultural backgrounds in music selection and program design to avoid appropriation or misrepresentation.
- Professional Competence: Ensure that music therapists and facilitators are adequately trained, certified, and adhere to ethical guidelines in their practice.
- Evaluation and Accountability: Regularly evaluate program outcomes and solicit feedback from participants and stakeholders to continuously improve program effectiveness and ethical standards.

Implementing music interventions in various settings requires a strategic approach that considers specific goals, participant needs, and ethical considerations. By leveraging the therapeutic potential of music, these programs can promote healing, enhance learning, foster community engagement, and improve workplace dynamics. Through careful planning, collaboration with stakeholders, and ongoing evaluation, music interventions can have a meaningful and lasting impact on individuals and communities alike.

11.7. Evaluating Program Success in Creating Therapeutic Music Programs

Creating therapeutic music programs involves designing interventions that leverage music's healing properties to address emotional, cognitive, and physical needs. Evaluating the success of these programs is crucial to understanding their impact on participants' well-being and optimising their effectiveness. Here is a detailed guide on how to evaluate the success of therapeutic music programs:

11.7.1. Importance of Evaluation

- Assessment of Therapeutic Outcomes
  - ✓ Determine the extent to which the program achieves its therapeutic goals, such as reducing anxiety, improving mood, enhancing social skills, or managing pain.
- Quality Improvement
  - ✓ Identify strengths and weaknesses in program design, implementation, and delivery to enhance program effectiveness and participant satisfaction.
- Demonstrating Impact
  - ✓ Provide evidence to stakeholders, including funders, healthcare providers, and participants, to justify continued support and funding for the program.
- Ethical Considerations
  - ✓ Ensure that evaluation methods respect participants' privacy, confidentiality, and cultural sensitivities while gathering meaningful data.

11.7.2. Key Evaluation Methods

- Quantitative Measures
  - ✓ Pre-Post Assessments: Conduct standardised assessments before and after program participation to measure changes in participants' symptoms, behaviours, or skills.
  - ✓ Behavioural Observations: Use structured observation protocols to document participant behaviours during music sessions, focusing on engagement, emotional expression, and interaction.

- ✓ Psychometric Scales: Administer validated scales (e.g., Beck Anxiety Inventory, Quality of Life Scale) to quantify changes in specific therapeutic outcomes related to mental health or quality of life.

- Qualitative Methods

✓ Participant Interviews: Conduct semi-structured interviews to explore participants' subjective experiences, perceptions of benefits, and challenges encountered during the program.

✓ Focus Groups: Facilitate group discussions with participants to gather collective insights on program impact, satisfaction levels, and suggestions for improvement.

✓ Case Studies: Compile detailed case studies of individual participants to illustrate specific therapeutic journeys, highlighting notable improvements or challenges.

- Programmatic Indicators:
  - ✓ Attendance and Engagement Rates: Track attendance records and participant engagement levels to assess program accessibility, retention, and participant commitment.
  - ✓ Participant Feedback: Collect ongoing feedback through surveys, questionnaires, or informal feedback forms to gauge participant satisfaction and identify areas for program enhancement.
  - ✓ Progress Notes: Maintain detailed progress notes and session logs to document individual participant progress, changes in treatment goals, and adjustments in therapeutic strategies.
- Comparison Groups
  - ✓ Controlled Studies: Conduct controlled studies with randomised controlled trials (RCTs) or matched control groups to compare outcomes

between participants receiving the therapeutic music intervention and those not receiving it.

11.7.3. Steps in Evaluation

- Establish Clear Objectives:
  - ✓ Define specific therapeutic goals and measurable outcomes aligned with the program's mission and the needs of the target population (e.g., patients with chronic pain, children with developmental disabilities).
- Develop Evaluation Plan
  - ✓ Design a comprehensive evaluation plan outlining evaluation methods, data collection tools, timeline, and responsibilities of evaluation team members.
  - ✓ Customise evaluation tools and protocols to accommodate diverse participant needs, cultural backgrounds, and communication preferences.
- Collect and Analyze Data
  - ✓ Implement data collection methods systematically throughout the program implementation phase, ensuring consistent monitoring of participant progress and program fidelity.
  - ✓ Analyse quantitative data using statistical software to identify significant changes in therapeutic outcomes and explore correlations between program variables and participant responses.
  - ✓ Interpret qualitative data through thematic analysis to uncover common themes, patterns, and participant narratives that illustrate program impact and participant experiences.
- Report and Utilise Findings

✓ Prepare a comprehensive evaluation report summarising findings, including quantitative results, qualitative insights, and participant testimonials.

- ✓ Disseminate evaluation findings to key stakeholders, including program staff, healthcare providers, participants, and funding agencies, using clear and accessible formats.
- ✓ Utilise evaluation findings to inform programmatic decisions, such as program modifications, expansion plans, funding proposals, and strategic partnerships.

11.7.4. Ethical Considerations in Evaluation

- Informed Consent: Obtain informed consent from participants or their legal guardians regarding participation in evaluation activities, ensuring clarity on the purposes of data collection, confidentiality, and the voluntary nature of participation.
- Confidentiality and Privacy: Safeguard participant confidentiality by anonymising data, storing it securely, and limiting access to authorised personnel only.
- Cultural Sensitivity: Respect cultural norms, values, and beliefs when designing evaluation methods, interpreting results, and disseminating findings to ensure relevance and sensitivity to diverse participant backgrounds.
- Participant Well-being: Prioritise participant well-being throughout the evaluation process, demonstrating empathy, respect, and support during data collection and feedback sessions.

Evaluating the success of therapeutic music programs requires a thoughtful and systematic approach that integrates both quantitative and qualitative methods, tailored to the program's goals and the needs of participants. By effectively measuring therapeutic outcomes, gathering meaningful participant feedback, and adhering to ethical guidelines, program managers can demonstrate the impact of their programs, inform evidence-based practices, and continuously improve program delivery to maximise therapeutic benefits for participants.

12 | DIY Music Therapy Techniques

Music therapy encompasses a range of techniques that utilise music to address physical, emotional, cognitive, and social needs. While professional music therapists undergo extensive training, there are several DIY techniques that individuals can incorporate into their daily lives for personal well-being and relaxation. Here are some effective DIY music therapy techniques:

12.1. Music Listening

- Purpose: Listening to music can evoke emotions, reduce stress, and promote relaxation.
  - ✓ Technique: Create personalised playlists: Curate playlists based on your mood or desired emotional state (e.g., upbeat for energy, calming for relaxation).
  - ✓ Mindful Listening: Focus on the music's rhythm, melody, and lyrics to enhance mindfulness and reduce anxiety.
  - ✓ Active Listening: Engage deeply with the music by paying attention to its nuances and emotional impact.
  - ✓ Benefits: It improves mood, reduces stress levels, enhances concentration, and promotes emotional expression.

12.2. Singing and Vocalisation

- Purpose
  - ✓ Singing and vocalisation can release tension, improve breathing, and foster self-expression.

- Technique
  - ✓ Singing Along: Sing along with your favourite songs or melodies that resonate with you emotionally.
  - ✓ Improvisational Singing: Create spontaneous melodies or hum tunes to express inner feelings and thoughts.
  - ✓ Chanting of Mantras: Repeat calming phrases or affirmations in rhythm with soothing music.
  - ✓ Benefits: It boosts mood, strengthens respiratory muscles, encourages creativity, and enhances emotional release.

12.3. Playing Musical Instruments

- Purpose: Playing instruments can improve coordination, enhance cognitive function, and provide a creative outlet.
- Technique: Learn a New Instrument: Start learning a musical instrument that interests you, whether it is guitar, piano, drums, or any other.
- Jamming Sessions: Play along with backing tracks or collaborate with others in informal music sessions.
- Improvisation: Experiment with spontaneous musical ideas to express emotions or relieve stress.
- Benefits: It enhances fine motor skills, stimulates brain activity, fosters self-expression, and promotes relaxation.

12.4. Songwriting and Lyric Analysis

- Purpose: Songwriting and lyric analysis can facilitate emotional processing, self-reflection, and personal growth.
- Technique

- ✓ Write Personal Songs: Create lyrics or compose music that reflects your experiences, emotions, or aspirations.
- ✓ Journaling with Music: Write about feelings and insights triggered by specific songs or lyrics.
- ✓ Discuss Lyrics: Analyse and interpret song lyrics that resonate with you, exploring their meaning and emotional impact.
- ✓ Benefits: It promotes self-awareness, enhances emotional expression, supports cognitive processing, and encourages creativity.

12.5. Movement to Music

- Purpose: Movement to music combines physical activity with rhythmic stimulation to improve coordination and mood.
- Technique
- ✓ Dance Therapy: Engage in freestyle dancing or structured dance movements to music that energises or relaxes you.
- ✓ Body Percussion: Create rhythms using body movements, clapping, or tapping along with music.
- ✓ Yoga with Music: Practice yoga poses or stretches synchronised with calming music to enhance relaxation.
- ✓ Benefits: It increases physical fitness, reduces stress levels, enhances coordination, and promotes emotional release.

12.6. Guided Imagery and Music (GIM)

- Purpose: GIM combines music listening with guided imagery to facilitate relaxation, emotional exploration, and personal insight.
- Technique

- ✓ Visualisation: Listen to instrumental music while guided through imagery or storytelling that promotes relaxation and mental imagery.
- ✓ Reflective Journaling: Write about the imagery, emotions, or insights experienced during the music session.
- ✓ Self-Guided GIM: Use pre-recorded guided imagery sessions with music or create your own scenarios to explore inner landscapes.
- ✓ Benefits: It facilitates deep relaxation, supports emotional processing, enhances self-awareness, and encourages creative visualisation.

12.7. Tips for Incorporation

- Consistency: Dedicate regular time to music therapy techniques to experience cumulative benefits over time.
- Personalisation: Customise techniques based on your preferences, emotional needs, and desired outcomes.
- Environment: Create a comfortable and distraction-free space conducive to relaxation and self-expression.
- Reflect and Adjust: Reflect on your experiences and adjust techniques as needed to maximise their therapeutic benefits.

Incorporating DIY music therapy techniques into your routine can provide significant emotional, physical, and cognitive benefits. Whether as a form of relaxation, emotional release, or creative expression, these techniques empower individuals to harness the therapeutic power of music in their daily lives.

12.8. Simple Practices for Home Use

- Deep Breathing with Music: Choose calming music with a slow tempo. Sit or lie down comfortably, close your eyes, and focus on your breath. Inhale deeply for a count of four, hold for four, and exhale for four, syncing your breath with the music's rhythm. This can help reduce stress and promote relaxation.

- Active Listening: Select a piece of music you enjoy and actively listen to it without distractions. Pay attention to the melody, harmony, and rhythms. Notice how the music makes you feel emotionally and physically. This practice enhances mindfulness and can improve mood.
- Rhythmic Movement: Use rhythmic music with a steady beat to engage in simple movements, such as clapping, tapping your feet, or swaying. This rhythmic activity can help improve coordination and motor skills while providing a sense of grounding and enjoyment.
- Creative Expression: Experiment with creating your own music using simple instruments, such as drums, shakers, or even household items like pots and pans. There is no need for musical expertise; the goal is to express emotions and release tension through sound.
- Music for Memory and Cognition: Use familiar songs or melodies to stimulate memory and cognitive function. Sing along to old favourites or play memory games where you recall song lyrics or titles. This practice can be especially beneficial for individuals with cognitive impairments.
- Music for Stress Relief: Create a personalised playlist of soothing music that helps you unwind. Play it during moments of stress or before bedtime to promote relaxation and better sleep quality.
- Improvised Singing: Singing can be therapeutic and does not require professional skill. Sing about your day, emotions, or anything on your mind. Improvised singing can be cathartic and help express feelings that are difficult to articulate.

- Guided Imagery with Music: Choose instrumental music that evokes a certain mood or setting (e.g., nature sounds, gentle piano). Close your eyes and imagine yourself in that environment while allowing the music to guide your mental imagery. This practice can enhance relaxation and visualisation skills.

These DIY music therapy techniques can be tailored to individual preferences and needs, providing accessible ways to incorporate music into daily life for therapeutic benefits.

12.9. Resources and Tools for Self-Directed Therapy

Exploring DIY music therapy techniques can be a powerful way to enhance mental well-being through self-directed therapy. Incorporating music into your self-care routine can provide relaxation, emotional expression, and stress relief. Here are some resources and tools to support your journey:

- Music Listening Apps: Platforms like Spotify, Apple Music, or YouTube offer extensive libraries of music across genres. Create personalised playlists tailored to your mood or therapeutic goals, such as calming music for relaxation or uplifting tunes to enhance your mood.
- Guided Music Meditations: Apps like Insight Timer and Calm feature guided meditations with music backgrounds. These sessions combine mindfulness techniques with soothing music to reduce stress, improve focus, and promote emotional balance.
- Music Therapy Websites and Blogs: Explore online resources dedicated to music therapy techniques and practices. Websites like the American Music Therapy Association (AMTA) provide information on therapeutic benefits, DIY techniques, and how music can support mental health.
- DIY Instrument Making: Engage in creating simple musical instruments at home using household items.

For example, you can make shakers with rice-filled bottles or drums using empty containers and balloons. Experimenting with these instruments can enhance creativity and provide a therapeutic outlet for self-expression.

- Online Music Therapy Courses: Platforms like Udemy or Coursera offer introductory courses on music therapy principles and techniques. These courses can provide foundational knowledge and practical skills for incorporating music into your self-directed therapy practice.
- Music-Based Relaxation Techniques: Learn techniques such as progressive muscle relaxation or deep breathing exercises accompanied by calming music. Websites like AnxietyBC offer free audio guides that combine relaxation scripts with soothing background music.
- Virtual Music Therapy Sessions: Some therapists offer virtual sessions where they guide individuals through personalised music therapy exercises via video calls. These sessions provide structured support and tailored techniques to help achieve specific therapeutic goals.
- Music Journaling Prompts: Use music as a source of inspiration for journaling prompts. Reflect on how certain songs or genres make you feel, memories associated with music, or lyrics that resonate with your emotions. Writing about your musical experiences can deepen your self-awareness and emotional processing.
- Community Music Groups: Join online communities or local groups focused on music-making or appreciation. Participating in virtual jam sessions, singing groups, or music discussion forums can foster connection, creativity, and a sense of belonging.

- Music-Based Self-Expression Workshops: Look for online workshops or webinars that explore creative ways to express emotions through music. These sessions may include songwriting workshops, improvisational music exercises, or therapeutic storytelling through music.

These resources and tools for self-directed therapy, utilising DIY music therapy techniques, provide diverse ways to incorporate music into your daily life for mental health benefits. Whether through listening, creating, or exploring new musical experiences, integrating music into your self-care routine can support emotional well-being and personal growth.

12.10. Case Studies of Self-Help through Music to Improve Their Well-Being

12.10.1. Case Study 1: Using Music for Stress Relief

- Background: Sarah, a 34-year-old marketing manager, experienced high levels of stress due to her demanding job and personal responsibilities. She often felt overwhelmed and struggled to relax after work.
- Approach: Sarah decided to incorporate music into her daily routine as a self-help tool for stress relief. She created a playlist of calming instrumental music and committed to listening to it during her commute and before bed. Additionally, she explored mindfulness techniques, synchronising her breathing with the music's rhythm to promote relaxation.
- Outcomes: Over several weeks, Sarah noticed significant improvements in her stress levels. The soothing music helped her unwind after busy workdays, facilitating a sense of calm and reducing tension. By integrating music into her self-care routine,

Sarah felt more equipped to manage stress and maintain a healthier work-life balance.

12.10.2. Case Study 2: Music Therapy for Depression

- Background: Mark, a 42-year-old teacher, struggled with persistent feelings of sadness and low energy associated with depression. He had tried medication and therapy in the past but was looking for additional strategies to support his mental health.
- Approach: Mark enrolled in a music therapy workshop focused on using songwriting as a therapeutic tool. Under the guidance of a music therapist, he explored his emotions through lyrics and melodies, expressing his experiences with depression in a creative way. He also learned relaxation techniques using music, such as guided imagery with calming instrumental pieces.
- Outcomes: Through regular participation in music therapy sessions and practising music-based self-expression techniques at home, Mark experienced notable improvements in his mood and emotional well-being. The act of writing and performing music provided an outlet for his feelings of sadness, helping him regain a sense of purpose and enjoyment in his daily life. Mark found that music therapy complemented traditional treatments and enhanced his overall mental health recovery journey.

These case studies illustrate how individuals have effectively utilised music as a self-help tool to address stress, enhance relaxation, and manage symptoms of depression.

13 | Future Trends in Psychosonic Research

By incorporating music into our self-care routines, we can achieve significant improvements in our emotional well-being and overall quality of life.

Psychosonic research explores the intricate relationship between sound, music, and psychological processes, paving the way for innovative applications in therapy, cognitive enhancement, and emotional well-being. As technology advances and interdisciplinary collaborations expand, several promising trends are emerging in this field:

- Neuroscientific Insights: Future research aims to deepen our understanding of how sound and music affect the brain at a neuroscientific level. Advances in neuroimaging techniques, such as functional MRI (fMRI) and electroencephalography (EEG), allow researchers to observe real-time brain activity in response to auditory stimuli. This insight can reveal the neural mechanisms underlying emotional regulation, memory formation, and cognitive functions influenced by music.
- Personalised Sound Interventions: With the rise of personalised medicine, there is a growing interest in developing customised sound interventions tailored to individual psychological profiles and therapeutic needs. Machine learning algorithms can analyse physiological responses, behavioural data, and preferences to prescribe music or soundscapes that optimise therapeutic outcomes. This approach holds

promise for personalised music therapy and stress management strategies.

- Virtual Reality (VR) and Augmented Reality (AR): Integrating soundscapes into VR and AR environments opens new possibilities for immersive therapeutic experiences. Future research may explore using virtual environments enriched with therapeutic soundscapes to treat anxiety disorders, PTSD, and phobias. These technologies can simulate calming natural environments or recreate soothing auditory stimuli to enhance relaxation and exposure therapies.
- Interactive Sound Installations: Interactive sound installations in public spaces or healthcare settings can promote mental wellness and community engagement. These installations may encourage active participation through music-making, collaborative soundscapes, or interactive performances. Future research will likely explore the impact of such installations on mood regulation, social connectedness, and stress reduction in diverse populations.
- Biofeedback and Sound Therapy Integration: Combining biofeedback techniques with sound therapy holds potential for enhancing therapeutic efficacy. Biofeedback devices can monitor physiological responses, such as heart rate variability or skin conductance, while sound interventions dynamically adjust in response to real-time data. This bioresponsive approach may optimise relaxation training, pain management, and emotional regulation therapies.
- Cross-Cultural Perspectives: As psychosonic research expands globally, there is increasing interest in understanding how different cultures perceive and utilise sound for healing and spiritual practices. Comparative studies on the role of music in cultural

rituals, traditional healing practices, and community bonding can enhance therapeutic approaches and foster cultural sensitivity in mental health interventions.

- Ethical Considerations and Accessibility: Future research will address ethical implications surrounding the use of psychosonic interventions, including privacy concerns, informed consent, and equitable access to sound-based therapies. Efforts to develop affordable, user-friendly technologies and ensure cultural appropriateness will promote inclusivity and ethical practice in psychosonic research.
- Future trends in psychosonic research are poised to revolutionise mental health care by harnessing the therapeutic potential of sound and music in innovative ways. From personalised interventions to immersive technologies and cultural insights, these advancements hold promise for enhancing emotional well-being, cognitive function, and quality of life across diverse populations.

This overview highlights the exciting possibilities ahead in the field of psychosomatic research, driven by advancements in technology, neuroscience, and a deeper understanding of the therapeutic potential of sound and music.

13.1. Emerging Areas of Study

Psychosonic research, which explores the intersection of sound, music, and psychological processes, continues to evolve with advancements in technology and interdisciplinary collaboration. Emerging areas of study within psychosonic research are shaping future trends and expanding our understanding of how sound influences cognition, emotion, and well-being. Here are some notable emerging areas:

- Neuroscience of Sound Perception: Advances in neuroscience are enabling deeper insights into how the brain perceives and processes auditory stimuli. Future research may focus on mapping neural pathways involved in music perception, emotional responses to sound, and the neural correlates of musical improvisation or creativity.
- Sound-Based Therapies for Neurological Disorders: There is growing interest in using sound-based therapies, such as rhythmic auditory stimulation and neurologic music therapy, for treating neurological disorders, including Parkinson's disease, stroke recovery, and traumatic brain injury. Research aims to elucidate mechanisms of neuroplasticity and motor rehabilitation facilitated by rhythmic auditory cues.
- Psychoacoustics and Spatial Sound Perception: Psychoacoustics examines how humans perceive sound spatially, encompassing factors such as localisation, distance perception, and sound field reproduction. Emerging research may explore immersive audio technologies (e.g., 3D audio, binaural recordings) and their applications in virtual environments, auditory displays, and therapeutic soundscapes.
- Music and Emotional Regulation: Studies continue to investigate the impact of music on emotional regulation and mood modulation. Future research may explore individual differences in emotional responses to music, the impact of specific musical features (e.g., tempo, harmony) on emotional states, and the therapeutic applications of music for managing mood disorders and anxiety.
- Interactive Sound Environments: Advances in interactive technologies and augmented reality (AR) are paving the way for interactive sound

environments that respond to user input or physiological signals. Future studies may investigate the therapeutic potential of interactive soundscapes for reducing stress, enhancing attentional focus, and promoting relaxation states.

- Cultural and Cross-Cultural Perspectives: Research in psychosonic studies is increasingly exploring how cultural backgrounds shape musical preferences, therapeutic practices, and the perception of sound-based interventions. Cross-cultural studies may examine diverse musical traditions, rituals involving sound, and cultural factors influencing the therapeutic efficacy of music.
- Biofeedback and Sound Interaction: Integrating biofeedback mechanisms with sound interventions holds promise for personalised therapeutic approaches. Future research may explore real-time physiological feedback (e.g., heart rate variability, skin conductance) to adapt therapeutic soundscapes and optimise stress management, pain relief, and emotional regulation therapies.
- Ethical and Accessibility Considerations: As psychosonic research advances, ethical considerations regarding privacy, consent, and equitable access to sound-based therapies are becoming increasingly important. Future studies will likely address ethical challenges and ensure culturally sensitive practices in the development and application of psychosonic interventions.

Emerging areas of study within psychosonic research are poised to advance our understanding of the therapeutic potential of sound and music across diverse applications. From neuroscience insights to interactive technologies and cultural perspectives, these areas of research will shape future trends in utilising sound to enhance psychological well-being and cognitive functions.

13.2. The Role of AI and Machine Learning in Music Therapy

AI (artificial intelligence) and machine learning are revolutionising various fields, and music therapy is no exception. These technologies offer innovative tools and approaches that enhance the therapeutic potential of music in addressing emotional, cognitive, and physical health challenges. Here are key ways AI and machine learning are transforming music therapy:

- Personalised Therapy Programs: AI algorithms can analyse large datasets of patient information, including preferences, physiological responses, and therapeutic outcomes. By processing this data, AI can recommend personalised music therapy programs tailored to individual needs and therapeutic goals. This approach ensures that interventions are more targeted and effective, optimising the therapeutic benefits for each client.
- Music Composition and Generation: AI-powered tools are capable of composing original music pieces based on predefined parameters, such as mood, tempo, and instrumentation. In music therapy, these compositions can be used to evoke specific emotional responses, facilitate relaxation, or engage clients in therapeutic exercises. AI-generated music offers therapists versatile resources for creating customised auditory experiences that support therapeutic objectives.
- Emotional Recognition and Feedback: Machine learning algorithms can analyse vocal intonations, facial expressions, and physiological signals to assess emotional states in real-time. In music therapy sessions, AI can provide therapists with feedback on clients' emotional responses to music, helping to refine

therapeutic interventions and enhance empathetic engagement.

- Interactive and Adaptive Therapeutic Tools: AI-driven interactive applications and virtual environments enable clients to engage actively in therapeutic activities, such as music improvisation, virtual reality (VR)-based music experiences, or interactive music-making sessions. These tools can adjust in real-time based on client interactions and responses, creating dynamic and engaging therapeutic experiences.
- Neuroscientific Insights: AI facilitates advanced analysis of neuroimaging data, providing insights into how music influences brain activity and neural pathways. Machine learning algorithms can identify patterns in brain responses to music, enhancing our understanding of neuroplasticity, cognitive functions, and the therapeutic mechanisms of music-based interventions.
- Data-driven Research and Evidence-Based Practice: AI enables music therapists to conduct data-driven research by analysing aggregated clinical data and outcomes. By identifying trends and correlations, AI supports evidence-based practice in music therapy, informing therapeutic protocols, treatment plans, and intervention strategies that are grounded in empirical evidence.
- Accessibility and Remote Therapy: AI-powered applications and virtual platforms make music therapy more accessible, particularly for individuals in remote or underserved communities. Telehealth solutions incorporating AI facilitate remote music therapy sessions, offering flexibility and continuity of care that is not limited by geographical constraints.

AI and machine learning are expanding the possibilities of music therapy by enhancing personalisation, therapeutic efficacy, and accessibility. These technologies empower music therapists with innovative tools to deliver more precise, responsive, and impactful interventions, ultimately improving the quality of life and well-being of clients through the therapeutic power of music.

13.3. Predicting Future Developments

Psychosonic research, which explores the interaction between sound, music, and psychological processes, is poised for significant advancements driven by technological innovation, interdisciplinary collaboration, and expanding applications in healthcare and beyond. Here are several key predictions for future developments in psychosonic research:

- Integration of AI and Machine Learning: Future research will increasingly leverage AI and machine learning algorithms to analyse complex datasets related to music perception, emotional responses to sound, and therapeutic outcomes. AI-powered tools will facilitate personalised music interventions tailored to individual preferences, physiological responses, and therapeutic needs, optimising treatment efficacy and client outcomes.
- Advancements in Neuroscientific Understanding: As neuroimaging techniques continue to evolve, future studies will deepen our understanding of how music affects brain structure, function, and connectivity. Research will explore the mechanisms of neuroplasticity, the neural correlates of emotional regulation through music, and the impact of musical training on cognitive abilities. These insights will inform targeted interventions for neurological disorders and mental health conditions.
- Innovative Therapeutic Applications: Emerging technologies such as virtual reality (VR), augmented reality (AR), and interactive sound environments will

expand the scope of therapeutic applications in psychosonic research. Virtual environments enriched with therapeutic soundscapes will offer immersive settings for treating anxiety disorders, PTSD, and chronic pain, enhancing therapeutic engagement and outcomes.

- Bioresponsive Sound Therapies: Advances in biofeedback technologies will enable the development of bioresponsive sound therapies that adapt in real-time to physiological signals such as heart rate variability, skin conductance, and brainwave activity. These personalised interventions will optimise stress management, emotional regulation, and pain relief, enhancing the efficacy of music-based therapies.
- Cultural and Cross-Cultural Perspectives: Future research will explore diverse cultural perspectives on music's therapeutic benefits, incorporating indigenous healing practices, rituals involving sound, and culturally specific musical traditions. Comparative studies will highlight cultural influences on music perception, emotional expression, and the therapeutic efficacy of music interventions across global populations.
- Ethical Considerations and Accessibility: As psychosonic research advances, ethical considerations surrounding privacy, consent, and equitable access to sound-based therapies will become increasingly important. Efforts to develop inclusive, culturally sensitive practices and technologies will promote ethical standards in research and clinical applications.
- Evidence-based Practice and Policy Impact: The accumulation of empirical evidence supporting the efficacy of music therapy and sound-based interventions will drive policy initiatives and healthcare integration. Future developments in

psychosonic research are anticipated to impact healthcare policies, guidelines for therapeutic practice, and educational curricula, thereby promoting a broader recognition of music's role in promoting mental health and well-being.

Future developments in psychosonic research are poised to revolutionise therapeutic approaches through technological innovation, neuroscientific insights, cultural perspectives, and ethical considerations. These advancements will enhance our understanding of the therapeutic potential of sound and music, paving the way for personalised, effective, and accessible interventions across diverse populations.

13.4. Conclusion

In Psychosonic: The Intersection of Music and Mental Health, the exploration of how music influences psychological well-being has illuminated profound insights and promising avenues for future research and application. This book has underscored the intricate relationship between sound, music, and mental health, revealing that music is not merely entertainment but a powerful therapeutic tool with transformative potential.

13.5. Summarising Key Insights

Throughout the book, we have explored the neuroscientific underpinnings of music perception, uncovering how various musical elements evoke emotional responses and stimulate neural pathways. From the rhythms that synchronise our movements to the harmonies that evoke profound emotional states, music has been shown to modulate mood, reduce stress, and enhance cognitive functions. The integration of AI and machine learning promises to revolutionise music therapy by personalising interventions and optimising therapeutic outcomes based on individual profiles and responses.

13.6. The Growing Importance of Music in Mental Health

As we look to the future, the role of music in mental health is poised to expand exponentially. With advancements in technology and a deeper understanding of neuroplasticity, music therapy will continue to evolve as a mainstream modality for treating neurological disorders, depression, anxiety, and trauma. The emergence of interactive sound environments, virtual reality therapies, and bioresponsive interventions heralds a new era where personalised, immersive music experiences will be accessible to all.

13.7. Final Thoughts and Call to Action

It is evident that the future of psychosonic research lies in embracing interdisciplinary collaboration, ethical practice, and cultural sensitivity. We must advocate for continued investment in research that explores the diverse therapeutic applications of music, from clinical settings to community interventions. Moreover, there is a pressing need to integrate music therapy into mainstream healthcare systems, ensuring equitable access and recognition of its profound impact on mental health outcomes.

As we conclude this journey through Psychosonic: The Intersection of Music and Mental Health, let us be inspired by the potential of music to heal, empower, and enrich lives. Let us champion policies that support the integration of music therapy into healthcare frameworks and educational programs. By embracing the transformative power of music, we can foster a healthier, more resilient society where every individual has the opportunity to thrive.

In closing, let us remember that in the symphony of life, music serves not only as a source of solace and joy but also as a beacon of hope and healing for generations to come.

9 789348 892799

Printed at Repro India Ltd.